Information Technology

The Management Challenge

The EIU Series

This innovative series of books is the result of a publishing collaboration between Addison-Wesley and the Economist Intelligence Unit. Our authors draw on the results of original research by the EIU's skilled research and editorial staff to provide a range of topical, information-rich and incisive business titles. They are specifically tailored to the needs of international executives and business education worldwide.

Titles in the Series

Information Technology

The Management Challenge

N. Caroline Daniels

The Economist
Intelligence Unit

▲▼ **ADDISON-WESLEY PUBLISHING COMPANY**

Wokingham, England • Reading, Massachusetts • Menlo Park, California • New York
Don Mills, Ontario • Amsterdam • Bonn • Sydney • Singapore
Tokyo • Madrid • San Juan • Milan • Paris • Mexico City • Seoul • Taipei

Cover designed by Pencil Box Ltd, Marlow, Buckinghamshire
incorporating photograph by Kerry Lawrence
and printed by The Riverside Printing Co. (Reading) Ltd.
Text designed by Valerie O'Donnell.
Line diagrams drawn by Margaret Macknelly Design, Tadley.
Typeset by Meridian Phototypesetting Limited, Pangbourne.
Printed in Great Britain at the University Press, Cambridge.

First printed 1993.   Reprinted 1994 and 1995.

ISBN 0-201-63195-4

British Library Cataloguing in Publication Data
A catalogue record for this book is available from the British Library.

Library of Congress Cataloging in Publication Data applied for.

Foreword

Understanding information technology (IT) is vital to every manager simply because IT is part of every manager's job. Managers in the 1990s must use IT to leverage their contributions to the organization, and they must be knowledgeable about IT so that they can lead others to do the same.

Today's organizations are becoming highly efficient and effective global entities facilitated both by their internal IT infrastructures and the increasingly integrated national and global IT infrastructures. This is the manager's new workplace. If the manager does not understand the new workplace, nor can work effectively in it, he or she faces quick obsolescence.

So, it is essential for the manager to substantively understand IT. This report provides a road-map for the manager who may not have grown up with IT to begin the journey of getting a grip on IT and becoming a 1990s manager of knowledge workers.

Dr Caroline Daniels has the right perspective to prepare this book for the manager. She has worked with leading-edge organizations, assisting their managements and executive teams to understand IT and to exploit its benefits when doing their jobs. She has also written thoughtful articles and books as well as carried out in-depth research and multi-client studies on subjects such as globalization, strategic information technology and organizational change. All of this effort has produced the latest research and practices in the management of IT. Her consulting experience coupled with her academic research experience has enabled her to write a unique, up-to-date book for the manager on this vital subject.

The manager will find that this book:

- balances theory and proven management frameworks and is illustrated with practical cases;

- explains in management terms the capabilities of IT in business;

- provides a good guide to managers who need to discover how to apply IT for strategic advantage.

Richard L. Nolan
Professor of Business Administration
Harvard Business School

Acknowledgements

Over the last few years I have spoken to hundreds of business and IT managers about their concerns in managing business information technology. The exploration has taken me to many different parts of the globe: to Singapore to view systems that have increased the port's advantage as a leading global shipping area; to California to see the latest software technologies; to Europe to view the latest developments in communications media. I have talked to many companies about their experiences.

Many people have had a hand in crafting this book. Carolyn White helped to shape the initial form of the ideas as well as to interest Addison-Wesley and the Economist Group in publishing the material. Jane Hogg has provided a steady supply of patience, sound judgement and an indefatigable supply of good nature for which I will continue to owe her considerably. Lynn Underwood played a determined editorial hand in transforming the material from a report into a book. Sarah Mallen worked on the alliance between the publishers and Wong Chiu Yin has expedited decision making so that the alliance could be forged.

I should especially like to thank the following companies for participating in the research: Apple Computer, Bankers Trust, Benetton, British Airways, the British Institute of Management, Club Med, Crédit Suisse First Boston, Deutschebank, Digital Equipment Corporation, Ford of Europe, International Business Machines, James River and Chartham Paper Mills, Mast Industries, Mercury International, Midland Bank, New York Life Insurance Company, Nissan, Norsk Hydro, Peat Marwick International, Rank Xerox, Scandinavia Airlines, SmithKline Beecham and Union Bank of Switzerland. Thanks also go to Sybil M. Baker and Lorraine M. Pitts for their help in the preparation of the material.

Dr N. Caroline Daniels

Contents

Executive summary

(1) Information technology allows companies to gain competitive advantage on a global basis. Regardless of size or market share, a key indicator of success in the future will be understanding how IT can integrate resources throughout a business.

(2) To understand how to take strategic advantage of IT, managers should chart the key information flows that support their business vision.

(3) Managing business information technology is like managing any other business asset. The key management decisions involve understanding the nature of the resource; allocating resources based on planning for benefits; and educating the workforce to use the technology.

(4) Involving key decision-makers in the design of IT systems is necessary to ensure that all shareholders understand the advantages to be gained with IT.

(5) Implementing an IT strategy requires a new management perspective that draws on available expertise both within and outside the firm.

(6) Encouraging a positive attitude towards technology commits and involves all employees in the search for competitive advantages achieved through IT.

(7) The competitive value of IT systems changes over time just as the business mission changes over time. It is important to integrate the development of the IT and business missions.

(8) Continuous learning through multimedia workstations enables employees to access powerful knowledge bases throughout the organization.

(9)   As technological change increases, managing the complexity of technology becomes more of a management responsibility. Business managers need to take the lead in the management of business information technology.

(10)   Major trends in global business are driven by information technology: new product development, sourcing, getting closer to customers and research.

IT and the global business environment

- Most businesses now have to compete in a global environment; a properly thought through IT strategy is essential to facilitate this.
- IT is far more than a technology to be mastered. Properly implemented IT can fundamentally change the nature of a business and the way it is managed.
- A prerequisite for a successful IT strategy is a global vision, both at the level of the firm and for industry and world business as a whole.
- In imposing common technical standards and funding IT research and development, governments can play a vital role in encouraging international business. A short-sighted protectionist stance can do long-term harm to their economies.

The challenge of IT

All over the world the way business is carried out is changing with the use of information technology. In virtually every industry, from banking and securities trading to manufacturing and design sectors, business managers are striving to harness the power of information technology. Leading international managers are now challenged to understand the impact of IT on their business. A leading business manager explained:

If you want to go into international business, you must have international communications systems. Electronic data interchanges are a necessity. Here, we especially need good global communications for engineering and product development. Understanding how IT can influence the way an organization operates internationally is vital. The new possibilities are important. Information flows provide the possibility to combine resources. Organizational changes are possible with IT.

Managing with IT involves understanding the implications for increasing the company's sphere of activity in the global marketplace, producing in the area of greatest advantage and distributing efficiently and effectively. All these processes are heavily dependent on the successful integration and management of IT within business objectives and practices.

Global changes to business are accelerating. For managers the pace of change can be difficult to track. Michael H. Spindler, chief executive officer of Apple Computer, Inc. said:

Today the dynamics of a truly global economy are destroying traditional concepts of time, geography, competition and strategic advantage. The challenge before us is to challenge our own thinking and to recognize that a global economy demands new structures, new management styles and new approaches to harnessing innovation. Globalization is in full swing in the world's capital movements, technology and market deployment. Perhaps no industry can match the transformation created by globalization like financial services. Using computer technology, a chief financial officer in Geneva or New York can track the cash flow of corporate divisions located around the globe. Investment portfolios and foreign exchange options can be monitored on a daily basis. The convergence of global competition, customized products and accessible technology has redefined the management practices of one of our more valuable resources: money.

It is also important to keep abreast of how companies are using IT around the world. The level of IT use in a country yields useful clues to the different marketplaces for products. Bjorn Boldt-Christmas, director of strategies at Scandinavian Airlines, described the importance of being really up-to-date:

It is important to know how different IT is in different parts of the world, taking note of the high technology aspects and how they could affect the business market. For example, if we know there are 5000 terminals in travel agencies in Sweden but only 60 in Greece, what does that say about the travel business in the respective countries? What can that tell us about our market?

It tells us that to arrange travel between Sweden and Greece requires a great deal of preparation, since plans will not be able to be changed easily. In Sweden there is a thriving economy which supports a large amount of business travel. To be a competitive player, IT is a must.

The biggest barrier to management's understanding of how to use IT is the perception that technology is somehow a force alien to business. Graham Gooding, director of systems at Ford Europe, described how he saw IT aligning with general management principles. He suggested that managers should 'relate the management of technology to the management of the business by drawing parallels between mainline business and business information systems' (see Management View 1).

Going global with IT

Whether a company is expanding into the global arena or protecting domestic markets from global competitors, business managers are more and more concerned with differentiating their businesses on a global basis. Figure 1.1 shows how a company changes when it becomes a global corporation. There are many powerful business reasons for going global and the following section demonstrates how IT must be an essential part of the strategy.

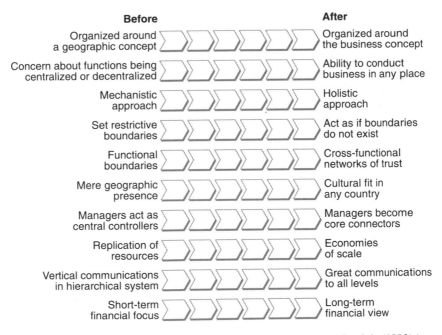

Before

	After
Organized around a geographic concept	Organized around the business concept
Concern about functions being centralized or decentralized	Ability to conduct business in any place
Mechanistic approach	Holistic approach
Set restrictive boundaries	Act as if boundaries do not exist
Functional boundaries	Cross-functional networks of trust
Mere geographic presence	Cultural fit in any country
Managers act as central controllers	Managers become core connectors
Replication of resources	Economies of scale
Vertical communications in hierarchical system	Great communications to all levels
Short-term financial focus	Long-term financial view

Figure 1.1   Becoming a Global Company. (*Source:* Daniels and Daniels (1993).)

Management View 1
Graham Gooding, Director of Systems, Ford Europe

Managing IT is essentially the same as managing any other discipline. Most managers are aware of the business issues relating to the products and services they produce for the market; now they have to transfer that management experience to understanding systems. Understanding business systems well is a very powerful source of strategic advantage and is based on the knowledge and experience of running the business.

Managers do not require an in-depth knowledge of computers or telecommunications to manage IT effectively. What they do need to understand is how IT can contribute effectively to achieving key business objectives – improved quality, reduced time to market, improved productivity – in their organizations. Managing IT for the first time can be an overwhelming experience for business managers because of the misunderstanding that the management principles for IT are vastly different from other management principles. Essentially, the management success factors are the same.

Implementation of any business objective is concerned with timely implementation and time to market. Similarly, efficient delivery of a new system is about timely implementation and time to market. Today's interest in simultaneous engineering is just as relevant to the efficient delivery of new systems. Managers are interested today in defining core business activities in all areas of the business, and this also applies to IT.

My advice to business managers beginning to deal with IT is to:

- filter out the buzz words
- ensure that key systems initiatives tie in to core business objectives
- build partnerships with your IT departments to achieve this.

The culture of a company flows through everything it does, so naturally the culture flows through the technology. Ford, General Motors and the Japanese makers all have different organizations built on decisions influenced by their unique cultures. Systems also reflect the culture of the organization. One of the largest issues is the development of the core skills of the company. At Ford we have a good dialogue with people from all over the company which enriches our skill base by knowledge transfer. The top management group is involved with the business decisions about IT.

Organizing around the business

As a business concept, a global company has a sphere of activity and awareness that stretches beyond where it operates to where it earns revenues, sources and carries out activities, or has a relationship with an outside party. IT plays a crucial role in helping managers to scan the environment for market and supplier intelligence, communicate findings and form communication links with business partners.

Global business managers leverage relationships with suppliers, distributors and customers cross-functionally and cross-geographically. Canon, of Japan, supplies products to many high-tech companies around the world; it also acts as distributor to many of these same companies within Japan. It expands its activities with one company by sharing the knowledge of its relationship with that company cross-functionally.

When producing world-class products with dependent technologies developing in different parts of the world, it is especially important to organize around the business rather than the function or geography. Managers of leading-edge companies are finding that activities which combine a cross-functional, cross-geographic approach produce benefits to the global corporation that are not normally found in the multinational corporation. Global market communications and global knowledge bases have broken down these barriers.

Doing business anywhere

Companies are moving from centralization/decentralization to 'anywhere'. Globalization is the ability to do business anywhere as opposed to worrying about which functions are centralized and which are decentralized. While most companies have yet to make the required investment, it is now possible for a company to wire the world in order to allow all its members to connect with each other as well as with outsiders.

DEC engineers in Augusta, Maine, call up CAD drawings on their terminals from a database in Reading, UK, update them and send them back in less than five minutes. Ford engineers in Cologne, Germany, examine and discuss a failed engine part with a Ford engineering team in south-east Essex, UK, using video-teleconferencing and an electronic blackboard, as well as facsimile. A high school science class in Texas can communicate with a robot submarine in the Mediterranean Sea to tell it where to point its video camera, while looking at the picture which is broadcast via satellite to multiple high school classrooms in the USA. Bond traders in London, Tokyo and New York watch multiple digital video inputs on their desks, talk on several different telephone lines to clients simultaneously, while all monitor an internal communication system. These are everyday, global occurrences. As Stan Davis says, it's an 'any time, any place' world (Davis, 1987).

The holistic approach

Companies must move their business orientation from mechanistic to holistic. A mechanistic view of the organization is one where the whole of the business equals the sum of its parts; a holistic organization is one where any part of the business reflects the whole culture of the business.

For employees global holism means the organization has shared beliefs, attitudes and values wherever the company chooses to do business. Real-time communication among employees to share ideas and activities fosters their commitment to the global corporate culture. This results in the consistency with which the company treats customers, vendors and other business partners.

At Benetton globalization can be seen in its product line (where it offers the same 3000 products worldwide), methods and advertising campaigns. The same United Nations/Colours/Contrasts of Benetton advertisements have become their global symbol. Underlying this is a global order entry and distribution system that allows Benetton to have its warehouse in Italy and deliver goods to any of its 5000 stores, anywhere in the world, within days.

Cross-functional coordination

Global companies act as if functional boundaries are low or do not exist. Recent research on Japanese manufacturing concerns indicates that they have an edge over US and European firms because they tend to coordinate cross-functionally better than their US counterparts (Abegglan and Stalk, 1985; Funk, 1988). Their low functional boundaries allow them to combine expertise to solve process issues. This coordination reduces the number of steps required to take action. Cross-functional relations promote the process orientation of IT systems. Management information systems are used to help manage the flow of work throughout operations.

The more complex a business, the more cross-functional coordination will help it. This benefit translates into reduced costs (by reducing steps in the process relating to hierarchic communication) and increased revenue (since resources are more flexible and can react more quickly to changes in market conditions). Task forces are organized around the purpose and process of the task, rather than strictly maintaining functional boundaries.

Working cross-functionally promotes a change from the 'not invented here' syndrome to networks of trust among employees who share information. Every individual in a network has what Peter Drucker (1988) calls 'information responsibility', that is, the responsibility to share relevant information with all others who have a need to know and not just assume that others should do the informing. By trusting the other people in the network employees reduce the amount of time and effort required to accomplish tasks.

Local good citizenship

Global companies have more than a geographic presence in a country or region. In moving from geographic presence to local good citizenship, companies are perceived by the local customers to have appealing characteristics. By using the information characteristics of global products and services, companies can differentiate these to reflect local culture and tastes to build local rapport.

The most obvious example of achieving local look and feel through the use of information is reflected in the ability to speak the customer's language. Apple Computer reaps huge benefits by providing keyboards and software packages that can adapt to local languages for its globally consistent personal computer processors.

Managers become core connectors

In a global business, the management core of the organization change their actions from central controllers to core connectors. They act as network nodes, as well as amplifiers and interpreters of the communications system. This is particularly the case in knowledge-worker dominated industries, where technical expertise is as valued as management expertise.

Economies of scale

Global IT can help companies move from replication of resources to economies of scale. One of the major economies of scale to be achieved is coordinating knowledge. For example, a large, highly successful consulting firm concentrates its IT investment on a central database of its client experiences, and makes this knowledge accessible around the globe. The partners and consultants see this as giving their company a powerful edge.

The networked organization

Companies becoming global also move from being stovepipes to having great communications. A company cannot be truly global without being wonderfully networked. In the fifteenth century, to the Portuguese or Spaniards, this may have meant having the fastest ships; today it means having great telecommunications and databases.

Management View 2
John L. Daniels, Vice President, Worldwide Business Transformation Consulting, IBM

Companies need to have a global vision to guide them in the creation of the global technology infrastructure. If they do not, the infrastructure costs are going to be too great and the time that it will take to build an adequate global IT platform will be too long. Global investments can be made in stages so long as the whole effort is in perspective.

A company's vision should reflect how it wants to support customers. This is likely to create the need for consistent business approaches around the world, while at the same time being highly responsive to local requirements. An effective company can provide service levels which match the customer requirements. A global IT plan that is centred around the requirements of global customers is one of the most important initial IT initiatives.

Companies are pretty good at devolving responsibility to national and local organizations in terms of letting the people develop their own support requirements. But they are not good at linking these different decentralized pieces together. Effective empowerment only comes when companies having an operating set of standard principles and guidelines that will allow the devolved activities to plug into each other to foster two-way communication. For example, many companies develop an accounting system to meet local requirements and then find out that they do not have a global chart of accounts. They cannot roll up information about the accounts. The definition of a sale, for instance, has to be consistent around the world so that a company can aggregate sales for a global customer. The problem that occurs when systems are developed on a completely decentralized basis is that one national organization is going to call a sale a sale when the customer places the order, another when the product is shipped, another when payment is made and so on. Global standards have to be met.

With increased international travel and communication there are many emergent global customer groups. Another reason why companies are trying to become global is because lifestyles are transcending national borders. Yuppies in Sweden have similar preferences to yuppies in France, Germany and Japan. They want to have the same kind of washing machine or car. This comes back to the global/local balance issues. While the Swedish and Japanese customers want the same products and services, they want them delivered within the context of their culture.

It is impossible to have a global IT infrastructure without adopting a philosophy that starts at the global business vision, is translated into business information requirements and gets driven down into the way that modules are developed to support operations at every level. That is how the whole global corporate mosaic is connected.

continues

continued

> Having a global IT plan enables executives and managers to put the picture together to envisage the future. A good IT planning process gives management a process and capability to describe a future state. To become global players managers have to live in the future to get to the future.

A global business is the embodiment of the networked organization, in that it has not one but multiple centres, located around expertise and competence. Communications need to be outbound and node-to-node as well as inbound.

Taking a longer-term view

Finally, leading companies are shifting from having only a short-term focus to having a long-term financial view. Effective strategic trade-offs can only be made if there is sufficient information to make global decisions. To enter a new market, it may be necessary to use cross-subsidies from other parts of the business rather than look for a one-year return on investment. Global IT can help to make the comparisons.

Organizing globally gives a business a wider picture of its inventory of ideas, skills and assets. A global management perspective gives a company the potential to integrate the business to provide global market solutions; to have an integrated culture based upon shared mindset, vision and values, while supporting local variations; and to leverage its learning and experience to develop the ability of learning how to learn.

Globalization is a competitive necessity that allows a company to keep up with the competition, keep abreast of new trends in technology and take advantage of developing business opportunity and risk. These objectives cannot be accomplished without IT.

Dynamics of national and global IT policy

Countries and regions are taking different approaches towards building global IT infrastructures. Not all governments have policies that encourage the spread of IT and only a few have recognized the advantages of a powerful communications infrastructure and taken steps to promote IT on a national and international basis. One country that has is Singapore, which has a National IT Plan with several important projects under way that will provide economic advantage (see Case 1.1).

Case 1.1   Singapore and Tradenet†

Context

Singapore, after 25 years of remarkable GNP growth at over nine per cent, has become the South East Asian country with the second highest standard of living behind Japan. GNP per head in 1990 was US$10,500. It has a population of approximately 2.7 m people and is located on a major world trade route on the southern tip of the Malaysian peninsula between the Pacific and Indian Oceans. Trade (exports and imports) through Singapore is three times the level of GDP and business leaders recognize that 'trade is our lifeblood'.

Why change?

Singapore's aim is to be a major strategic node for global business and to be recognized as a developed nation by the year 2000. Many progressive programmes have been initiated to achieve that end, one of the most important being the National IT Plan launched in 1985 (see Figure 1.2).

Singapore's leaders are counting on IT to provide future trade advantages, particularly to enable them to move upstream into more highly skilled, higher value-added, technology-intensive activities. The first project chosen by the government was to improve the operations of the Port of Singapore to make it the most effective port in the world. The improvements aimed to provide fast unload-load turnaround for container ships and high quality warehousing facilities, as well as associated distribution services.

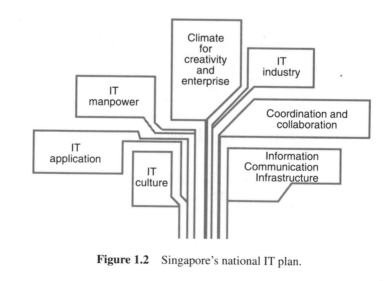

Figure 1.2   Singapore's national IT plan.

continues

continued

Vision

The Port of Singapore Authority formalized its vision as follows:

> Our corporate commitments are to our customers, to Singapore, to our employees, to a sound financial policy and to technical excellence. To our customers, we promise to meet their needs and provide them with value-for-money services promptly, reliably and efficiently. To Singapore, we accept our social responsibility to maintain a clean, safe marine environment which every Singaporean can enjoy. To our employees, recognizing them as our most important resource, we will provide a rewarding and challenging environment, with teamwork and good union-management relations, to help them realize their potential. In terms of financial policy, we believe in competitive pricing and effective cost control to earn a reasonable return to finance our growth. In technological excellence, we will use the latest port and information technologies to gain competitive advantage.

What the authority did

Singapore is an *entrepôt* for trade between East and West and is one of the world's busiest ports. Over 30,000 ships of 700 shipping lines from 80 countries use the port annually. It also prides itself on being a 'one-stop shipping centre', providing dry-docking, ship repair, survey, bunkering and ship supply 24 hours a day, 365 days a year.

Tradenet was put in place to help ships pass through the port in as short a time as possible. It is an electronic interchange system that links the Port Authority with government agencies, traders, transport companies, shipping lines, freight forwarders and airlines. The system facilitates on-line information transfer to reduce documentation and the transit time of cargo.

As the ship arrives in port, the shipper enters the cargo details into the system and transmits them through the Port Authority to the appropriate government trade and customs agencies for clearance. The format for the information the agencies require has been reduced to one common document. For the shipper this means that one submission via Tradenet can take care of all trade and customs requirements. The system can process the documentation and get the appropriate approvals in 15 minutes, rather than the two days taken previously.

Outcome and future

The benefits to shippers have been substantial. The predictability of their trade routes has become more stable. As a result interdependent issues such as inventory management and problems caused by delays can be averted.

The improvement in the effectiveness of operations has enabled the port to process more trade than ever before. Singapore has recently overtaken Hong Kong and become Asia's largest container shipping port. Singapore Network Services, the guardian of the project, plans to extend the system and is considering marketing it to other ports around the world.

Protectionism hinders global business

An important issue with which individual countries and regions are in the process of coming to grips is the paradox that unique standards, which on the one hand provide a protectionist environment for domestic businesses, can actually hinder the development of global business. Governments that hold out for a unique standard may well be isolating their countries from the commercial flow of the world. For example, the government of Brazil has set a mandate that allows only computers which have been manufactured in Brazil to be used. While the mandate has undoubtedly helped the development of some high technology manufacturing sectors in Brazil, the business system as a whole has been held back by limiting the number of IT products available, and limiting their improvement and development through contact with leading technologies from other countries.

The integration of European markets provides European countries with a stepping stone to globalization. While differences in standards and modes of business behaviour as well as IT systems will prevail well after formal integration, business managers are already learning valuable lessons in being able to connect and communicate between systems.

North America has opened up its telecommunications industry to more competition, allowing prices to be more competitively set as well as stimulating information companies to offer more services to help business.

Communications infrastructure is key

Pacific countries, which have to deal with long distances between customers, have long recognized the value of a communications infrastructure to economic growth. The four tigers – South Korea, Hong Kong, Taiwan and Singapore – enjoying the fastest recent economic growth in the area, have built up formidable linkages to other countries acting as a conduit for goods and services from the developing nations to the developed.

Developed and underdeveloped nations link knowledge and other resources via networks. Programmers in India provide programming support to American Express and other companies. For developing countries, communications infrastructures mean access to world markets and a way to keep in touch with developing world resources.

Infrastructure, the electronic highway of the information age, takes a significant time to build. The investment must be made over a period of years to allow business people to have time to learn how to run their businesses to take advantage of the changes in the IT infrastructure. Countries and regions that recognize the importance of a world-class communications infrastructure are giving their companies an unrivalled advantage in global business.

Action checklist

Reviewing the following questions about your business will help clarify the future of your IT strategy:

(1) What are the international barriers that your company faces in the global business arena? Are these imposed by the company itself?

(2) Does the company have connections outside the company, for example with suppliers and customers, on an international basis?

(3) Do your global customers want consistent products and services that also vary in some respects from local area to local area? Can the information content of the service offered be altered to provide this localization?

(4) Are your managers planning and using IT for a global future?

(5) How important is information in reaching your company's objectives?

References

Abegglen, J. and Stalk, G. (1985). *Kaisha: the Japanese Corporation*, New York: Basic Books

Daniels, J. L. and Daniels, N. C. (1993). *Global Vision: Building New Models for the Corporation of the Future*. New York: McGraw-Hill

Davis, S. (1987). *Future Perfect* (entitled *2001* in some countries). Reading, Massachusetts: Addison-Wesley Publishing Company Inc.

Drucker, P. (1988). The Coming of the New Organisation. *Harvard Business Review*, **66**, (1), January–February

Funk, J. L. (1988). How Does Japan Do It? *Production*, August

† This case was prepared from interviews; material was provided by Singapore's National Computer Board and the Port of Singapore Authority; the Harvard Business School case 'Singapore Tradenet: A Tale of One City' was prepared by John King; and from viewing the videotape 'The Intelligent Island' produced by Pat Greenland of the BBC

2

Frameworks for thinking about business and IT

- One of the most critical ways IT affects business is in changing the relationship between suppliers and customers, in many cases enabling a more individual and personalized contact.

- An effective IT strategy can encourage the development of new products and businesses.

- IT investment is never static; it must be constantly monitored and upgraded to secure maximum competitive advantage.

- To analyse the level of IT investment necessary for your firm you should undertake an audit of your information requirements now and in the future.

- A key management issue is to realize that IT is fundamentally process-related, and will change the nature of job functions throughout an organization.

Affecting the nature of competition

The previous section described some of the characteristics of a global company, and how the process of going global is critically dependent on IT. IT, however, is far more than a new business tool to be learnt and mastered. Its evolution has created an independent business force to be recognized and measured.

Michael Porter, Harvard Business School professor and eminent author in the field of business strategy, has written that 'the information revolution is affecting the nature of competition in three vital ways':

- It changes industry structure and alters the rules of competition ... by increasing the power of buyers, raising barriers to entry, and influencing the threat of substitution.
- It creates competitive advantage by giving companies new ways to out-perform their rivals ... by lowering costs, enhancing differentiation and changing competitive scope.
- It spawns whole new businesses, often from within a company's existing operations ... by making new businesses technologically feasible, creating derived demand for new products and creating new businesses within old ones (Porter and Millar, 1985).

Changing industry structure

Changing the structure of an industry involves changing the premises on which companies compete, in particular the ways that customers buy from companies and suppliers interact with buyers. In the retail banking industry, for example, a wide network of branch offices was initially an advantage in reaching the market. Today the network of physical branches may prove to be detrimental to business, since it represents a huge capital outlay for relatively unproductive assets. The real networks supporting the industry are now IT-based. An extreme example is First Direct, a Midland Bank initiative, which allows cus-tomers to telephone for service on their accounts at any time, with reduced rates during off-peak hours. Thus customers calling at 2 a.m. can have access to a customer service representative who will guide them through their information requests.

Customers are increasingly requesting that products be customized to their needs. Modifying the information content of products and services is a flexible way to respond to the market that IT can easily facilitate. For example, in the brick manufacturing industry it is becoming increasingly important to be able to make the style and size of brick to the quantity ordered. During boom periods of business, customization attracts a larger market share. During periods of economic downturns, increasing a company's ability to produce to specification can keep costs down.

In the UK, Steetley Building Products's Parkhouse brickworks produces 1.6m bricks each week in a fully automated plant. The order-handling system is used to increase flexibility by scheduling brick production. Inventory build-up and backlog have been virtually eliminated (Bradshaw, 1990). Architects can connect their building designs and interpret the brick requirements into the Steetley brick design system. The customer's system and the producer's system connect with Steetley's manufacturing process to produce accurate, volume-balanced orders.

In another business British Airways has invested heavily in customer information databases. Management data include market share, seats filled, on-time delivery, baggage statistics, passenger satisfaction and other service indicators. This information is received monthly by the directors of marketing and operations and 250 top BA managers. By improving its attention to customers' needs BA fills more seats than most airlines; its success is based on a yield-management system called Cobra (Holberton, 1990; Tilley, 1990).

Ship-making companies in the UK use computer-aided design as a tool to allow customers to inspect an image model of a ship and change certain design features before the ship is made. This use of computer models to replace prototype building or building a standard and adding features, gives companies a further dimension to customer responsiveness. The companies can design a different ship for each customer if desired. Once the design is set, the computer can generate the building drawings.

Insurance companies are using image systems to replace paper-driven processes. The customers benefit from agents having readily available, accurate, up-to-date information. The agents appreciate the ability to confirm the acceptance of a policy in the customer's home. The delay caused by communicating back and forth to head office used to result in missed opportunities for closing the sale. 'Customers are more apt to commit themselves if they have the option to sign when they have made the first purchase decision,' an agent recounts.

Managers must balance the application of IT to customers with the appreciation customers have for IT. Many customers do prefer to be treated to 'high-tech/high-touch' approaches such as talking to a customer service representative who is supported by powerful information systems. Others, however, still refuse to use automatic teller machines at banks, preferring the human interface.

Gaining and keeping repeat customers is increasingly competitive and expensive. Various studies indicate that repeat customers are the most profitable for companies, that customers are increasingly exercising their option for choice, and that the cost of gaining back a lost customer is five times that of keeping customers happy. As companies have more access to information to tailor their offerings and streamline costs, the level of information management needed to maintain parity also increases. Since putting systems into play can take three to five years, the sooner managers explore the importance of understanding the ways customer information can affect their relative position in business the better.

Depending on how the players in an industry manage their business information, the relative power of buyers and suppliers can shift. Buyers can improve competitive positioning by condensing purchasing information to compare suppliers more easily. Many buyers are reducing the number of suppliers they manage by focusing on managing a few suppliers very well. In Europe, with the integration of markets, many companies are rationalizing their supply base and distribution chains. Ford Europe is in the process of linking to suppliers to reduce the inventory of parts carried, and to decrease the time to delivery by eliminating paper. Reducing the number of suppliers allows the company to focus its information management resources to improve management of the supplier base. In addition, barriers to entry become higher if the management of information between existing buyers and suppliers reinforces the business relationship.

Changing the industry structure creates competitive advantage for the companies that lead the change and can have devastating effects on slow-moving companies that fail to react. But not all systems that create competitive advantage necessarily change the industry structure, as the examples in the next section reveal.

Creating competitive advantage

The second item in Porter's framework shows how understanding IT can help managers create competitive advantage. Not every system is expensive, grand and glorious. Systems that contribute to competitive advantage have in common that they are designed and applied to reduce costs, enhance differentiation or change competitive scope.

Boeing, the world's leading civil aircraft manufacturer, has built a modest but effective system for sorting drill bits, crucial to the production of aircraft. Over 600 types of drill bits are used to drill hundreds of thousands of holes in each aeroplane. The company has over 5m drill bits. Previously all of the used bits were sorted by six full-time labourers. Boeing designed an automated sorting process at a cost of $800,000 that has saved $500,000 in lower error rates, labour and related costs during the first eight months of operation (Abrahams, 1990). By lowering Boeing's costs, the system has freed financial and human resources to work on other business issues.

BMW is attempting to save two years in the design process and enhance differentiation by a combination of moving designers into a building that facilitates face-to-face communication and the use of leading-edge computer-aided design systems. The company hopes to extend the benefits to the manufacturing process by linking design and manufacturing systems to produce a simultaneous engineering system which will develop manufacturing methods in line with the designs (Griffiths, 1990).

Toyota operated a sophisticated Kanban production control system for years without the use of computers. The management of information in its just-in-time process facilitated huge reductions in costs and increases in speed of delivery. The company is now computerizing the process, as the early years of its competitive advantage are past and a faster, more complex system which gives real-time delivery is needed. This illustrates the point that understanding the information content of business processes is a prerequisite to developing IT systems that deliver advantage.

Kanban

Kanban in Japanese means 'record card'. It was developed by the car industry in Japan as the first 'just-in-time' method: in other words, a completely manual system of planning and control of materials and production time. Two types of cards are used – one which gives permission for something to be moved and another which gives permission for action. For example, a movement Kanban might be attached to a materials bin which is then moved to the stores and an action Kanban is attached which signals that that bin should be refilled with parts. The action Kanban is removed, the parts put in the bin and another movement Kanban attached. It is simple, but effective.

Rolls-Royce, a company that takes pride in the 'hand-crafted' quality of design, has turned to IT to take time out of the design cycle. Alternative design criteria are considered using computers to generate drawings and to perform assessments of the end product. The computers take some of the designers' work and perform it more quickly leaving them free to concentrate on the creative aspect of designing the unique quality of the cars. This practice begs the question: what is hand-crafted? To be hand-crafted, does the designer have to make every calculation without the aid of a computer? Rolls-Royce is integrating the capabilities of people with computers in the design activity. The company expects to decrease product development time by a year, generating estimated savings of £13m (Cookson, 1990).

Levi-Strauss, the world's largest clothing manufacturer, uses a line-balancing system in its Whitburn, Scotland, factory to manage production. In other words by planning production in line with demand the peaks and valleys of production activity are spread over time. This is part of the company's effort to create a global real-time production control system. One of the features of the system enables workers to calculate their income by piecework. It also allows them to schedule themselves, thus leaving management with more time to concentrate on non-supervisory work (Cookson, 1990). Eventually management would like to connect ordering systems with production systems so that the company can produce new products to order rather than forecast.

Spawning new businesses

The third item in Michael Porter's framework for the ways IT can affect the strategy of a firm is creating new business opportunities. The classic case is Merrill Lynch's creation of the cash management account (CMA) in the late

1970s. As banking regulations began to change in the USA, the management of the company saw an opportunity to merge certain products – cheque account, charge card and brokerage service – into one. The crux of the development of the new product was to integrate customer account information in a way flexible enough to enable the customer to increase the currency of funds, and at the same time reward the customer for keeping funds in the account. Merrill Lynch was able to manipulate information by customer, rather than account type, as did most of its financial competitors. Within five years the company captured the lion's share of the market, opening 5000 accounts per week and holding 70% of the market with 915,000 accounts. Its competitors took a few more years to catch up.

Reuters Holdings plc has become the world's leading electronic publisher by creating a whole new range of products through providing information services. Continuous technical innovation has helped the company to generate over 65% of 1989 revenue of £1.2bn through real-time information products such as up-to-the-minute worldwide news information and up-to-date information on stock prices. Reuters has become the world leader in providing stock market information as markets have become electronic.

American Express created demand for its Gold Card by altering the product to offer information as well as credit. The company targeted high income customers who want a great deal of detail on business and travel expenses. Gold Card customers can now get a summary of their account expenditures at the end of the year, thus providing instant answers to expense queries: a great help for busy executives.

Perhaps the best illustration of the power of IT to transform businesses occurred in the late 1970s and early 1980s, when Bob Crandall, CEO of American Airlines, announced that the company was becoming the 'high technology' airline. A competitor, Don Burr, president of People's Express, thought: 'What does he mean by that, what is high tech about an airline company?' Within months Mr Burr had his answer: the American Airlines Sabre (Semi-Automated Business Research Environment) system gave it a powerful advantage by providing management with information about seat reservations, such as the number of seats filled, price variations and customer details. More importantly, Sabre brought with it the capability to manipulate this information in split seconds, thus beginning a discount ticketing system that met every customer demand. American Airlines could beat any competitor's fare, any time, any place – and did so.

American Airlines then offered the use of the system to travel agents so that they could make their own bookings for their customers. Agents liked the system because they could manipulate information with ease and flexibility, perusing rate charts for the best offers and making the reservation in real-time while the customer sat in their office or chatted over the telephone. The agents improved their responsiveness to their customers by using Sabre. Sabre was able to forge a powerful interorganizational link between independent agents and American Airlines.

Much of the competition could not react fast enough. Don Burr had already made the decision not to invest in information systems. His airline's management team invested in what they considered to be their core business: flying aeroplanes. They had not considered information as key to the business.

By the time airlines such as People's Express realized what an advantage manipulating information about flight schedules, fares and their customers could be, it was too late. Even if they reacted quickly they could not equal the investment in time and money that for years American Airlines had put into its IT infrastructure. People's Express was eventually sold to a competitor. Being blind to the potential use of customer and other business information cost Mr Burr the company. Competitive advantage in the airline industry turned out to be as much about IT as about aeroplanes.

IT plays many roles in business:

- automating existing processes
- building communications infrastructures both within the company and externally
- linking to the company's customers and suppliers
- providing tools that extend the knowledge and capacities of designers
- supplying decision support
- quickly calculating huge droves of information.

How the competitive value of IT changes over time

The story of American Airlines illustrates another important aspect of IT: the competitive value of IT changes over time. Leaders who initiate the use of IT at one level of opportunity are quickly imitated by their competitors.

The initiatives that Bob Crandall and Max Hopper developed with IT are now part of the ground rules for competing in the airline industry:

- practising yield management (maximizing revenue by manipulating the allocations of seats)
- creating Super Saver fare programmes to pull customer demand
- using Frequent Flier programmes to attract and keep loyal customers.

These three competitive management practices are facilitated and enhanced by using IT to manage complex data in an elegant way. Crandall and Hopper understood the value of business information to their industry.

Competitive progression

In other industries the same phenomenon exists (see Figure 2.1). In banking the early stages represented the bank's ability to process cheques and produce informative statements for customers. Moving to a time when the cost of labour was increasing in relation to the amount of service customers required,

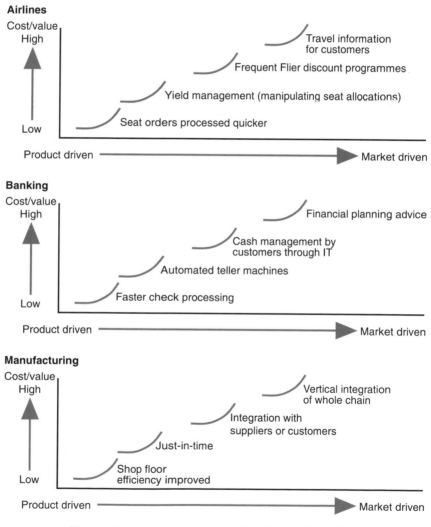

Figure 2.1   Competitive progression of certain industries.

the banks responded with the technological solution of automated teller machines (ATMs). Soon, however, the simple ATM was replaced by more sophisticated information systems that allowed customers to interact with the system, to manipulate funds into various savings and cheque accounts and to pay bills directly. This investment in technology allows the service personnel to concentrate on giving a more personalized service to the customer by offering financial planning advice, while knowledge databases assist the service officer with product and service information. Some banks provide customer access to their own accounts to display and consider portfolio scenarios.

Manufacturing industries show the same competitive progression in the uses of IT. Competitive progression in manufacturing has moved from providing information on the shop floor, such as how much is produced in what amount of time, to providing integrated sales and product systems that tie customer desires closer to what the firm actually produces. With just-in-time manufacturing, suppliers linked to customers in order to gather precise information for reorder by studying the patterns of sales and usage. Some suppliers are now looking at the patterns of usage of the product not only to fulfil orders to their retail customers just-in-time, but also to notify their suppliers to provide materials to meet their customer needs. Industries are becoming linked, providing a vertical integration through electronic means from company to company.

Understanding the value of information

In the 1980s the opportunities for companies that managed information for competitive advantage were limited to companies that built their own systems. The emphasis has now shifted. Rather than understanding the technical aspects of IT, it is more important for business managers to understand the value and flow of the business information itself, and then to apply the technology with the help of technologists. The information challenge cannot be ignored because the roles of IT have expanded: a company's competitors' managers are probably increasing their understanding, and a lack of knowledge is more likely to hurt than it was before.

Management adeptness at using information is increasing as businesses become more market driven. As times change, the bases of competitive advantages change and so do IT systems. Customer values and desires in terms of quality and service are replacing other feature variations to differentiate many products and services. Manufacturers are striving to become more flexible in order to be able to predict the volume required rather than overproducing. Each of these requires the more accurate manipulation of the information content of the business processes. The role of IT, too, has changed from providing support to administrative functions (such as inventory and payroll) to enabling processes by capturing information and manipulating it into knowledge (such as capturing customer preference information and transforming it into a new product design).

Max Hopper believed the advantages of Sabre have changed drastically. In future, rather than gaining advantages by building technological links to customers, management must concentrate on the content of the information within the business processes and manage that well. 'Competition shifts from building tools that collect data to using generally available tools to turning data into information and information into knowledge' (Hopper, 1990). The advantage will come to companies whose managers understand the information flow of the business and how to manage that information into valuable knowledge, rather than those whose managers handle only the technology side of the business.

Sabre is now used on 85,500 terminals at travel agencies in 47 countries and 665 airlines use it for fares and schedules. The system has expanded to cover pricing and availability for more than 20,000 hotels and 52 car rental companies. Sabre calculates complex data relating to flight plans, aircraft weight, fuel requirements, cargo and baggage handling, crew scheduling and other variables for over 2250 flights a day. It also maintains an inventory of almost 1 bn spare parts for maintenance purposes. Sabre, now sold as a service to other airlines, hotels and car rental companies as a leading computerized reservation system (CRS), is a profit centre, and one of the most profitable parts of the company, while also supporting the company's operations (Labich, 1990).

In future Crandall and Hopper will look to the use of the knowledge created by CRSs to develop competitive advantages, rather than building the systems themselves.

Competitive advantages that information management generates change over time. The competitive progression of the uses of IT optimally meets the change in corporate strategies, which, in turn, meets changing market conditions and the changing visions of the executive team. George Stalk (1988), author of many works on time-based competition, noted the transient nature of advantage of any business process:

> Like competition itself, competitive advantage is a constantly moving target. For any company in any industry, the key is not to get stuck with a single simple notion of its source of advantage. The best competitors, the most successful ones, know how to keep moving and always stay on the cutting edge.

Thomson Holidays in the UK achieved a similar competitive progression of advantages through the use of information technology in the travel holiday business in Europe (see Case 2.1).

Case 2.1 Thomson Holidays

Context

International Thomson Organisation Ltd (ITOL), a multinational company controlling newspapers, publishing, North Sea oil and other global activities, entered the UK travel industry in the late 1960s. Attracted by the fact that Thomson Holidays would create a positive cash flow in the short-term and required a relatively low initial investment, ITOL's management looked to the new travel arm for long-term growth. The initial strategy would be to reduce prices as much as possible and go for volume, while offering better quality low-price holidays to consumers.

The holiday travel industry consists of four types of business:

- supply of travel (airlines, ferries, trains and coaches)
- provision of accommodation (hotels, flats, cottages)
- sales through tour operators (package providers)
- sales through travel agents, who talk directly to customers to fill the capacity of holiday products.

The management of the information supporting the industry required using manual card indexes which were labour-intensive, time-consuming and prone to error.

Why change?

Travel agents had to rely on telephone communication to the tour operators to close a sale to a customer. Booking by telephone created a time lag between the customer's decision to buy and the tour operator's confirmation of the order. During this time gap customers could change their minds about purchasing a holiday, which meant a loss of revenue to the industry as a whole. By the middle to late 1970s competitors were beginning to close this gap by introducing computers to improve speed and reliability and to cut administrative costs.

Vision

Thomson's management created a vision for the company: to provide top quality holidays for customers and to create a real-time linkage to agents to make it easier for them to book holidays with Thomson than with any other company.

What Thomson did

Colin Palmer, Thomson Holidays' sales director, was selected to lead the effort. As he says:

continues

---

continued

Pricing strategies will always be a major determining factor, but below the surface the battles in the travel business are being fought with a more subtle weapon, information technology (IT). Technology is now the basis of the travel business. Apart from computer systems, tour operators own very little. They buy beds and airline seats, put them together and market a holiday package. It is natural that they should look to technology to develop the business.

The five objectives for Thomson Open-line Programme (TOP), introduced in the UK in 1982, were as follows:

- Reduce administration costs and improve productivity to create a competitive edge with cost structure.
- Provide agents with high performance tools to link them directly to Thomson Holidays' booking system.
- Enhance Thomson Holidays' reputation among travel agents by having the best reservation system.
- Treat all agents equally, without giving special advantages to multiples.
- Provide a competitive edge for a year or so by having the leading-edge on-line reservation system.

Outcome

For travel agents TOP increased sales by closing the sales gap, improving client service and providing a more efficient booking system with an ability to plan sales, faster access to Thomson and leading-edge communication at reasonable rates. In 1989 92% of travel agents named Thomson as the operator providing the most efficient reservation system.

Thomson Holidays had captured 33% of the market; its closest competitor had 19%. In effect, by changing the cost structure of the industry, Thomson changed the pricing structure to the benefit of the consumer. Colin Palmer attributes the aggressive competitive strengths of Thomson Holidays to TOP: 'The reason that Thomson was able to strike out as aggressively as it did on pricing at the start of the 1989 summer programme (a make or not-make pricing war) was accumulated savings, put at some £28m, in administration costs that it had achieved through its use of IT in its reservation system.'

Future

A consortium of competitors is now meeting to take the next step in the competitive progression of IT in the travel industry. The Travel Technology Initiative (TTI) is a system designed to increase customer service. TTI enables travel agents to issue one standard ticket for travel – by air, ferry and train.

Thomson is also in planning mode. Brian Eatock, assistant director of Thomson, believes that: 'Where the magic comes through is in the management techniques. We always need to be looking for follow-on, looking to the future, thinking about how to update our five-year plan. The essence is to keep the business information technology in line with the business vision.'

Analysing a company's IT requirements

Managing IT is clearly critical to the development of most modern businesses. But it can mean a huge investment, and many executives are rightly sceptical of the cost and time involved. The first requisite in managing IT is to decide how much IT the company really needs. Warren McFarlan of the Harvard Business School has devised a strategic grid for thinking about how intensively an industry uses information (Figure 2.2), as it is the need to mani-pulate information that drives the level of IT investment required.

McFarlan's strategic grid

The grid relates dependence on IT systems to the impact of IT on a business. Some businesses such as airline industries manipulate large quantities of data with many different dimensions to manage their business from day to day. A major European airline recently calculated that if its reservations system were completely out of commission it would cost the airline £1m per hour. Companies that are highly dependent on the speed of access, complexity and

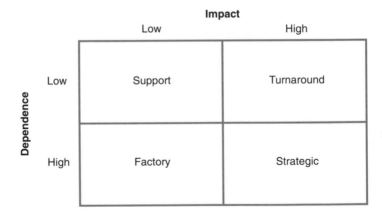

Figure 2.2   Strategic grid for positioning information systems in various types of company. (*Source:* Professor F. Warren McFarlan, *Harvard Business Review,* 98–103, May–June 1984.)

accuracy of information must make an extensive investment in information management to be competitive. The information systems in these cases are of strategic importance to the firm.

Businesses with low dependence on information may find that the loss of immediate access to information is annoying but can be managed. Many companies that have not automated extensively are not dependent on information, although perhaps they should be. A plumbing service company that holds accounts and customer service files on computer could operate for several days without its IT system. Manual back-up is achievable for businesses which are not complex. The information systems in this case play a supporting role.

Measuring the impact of information on a business is equally important. To position a company on this part of the grid it is necessary to ask if one of the top three agenda items for the company is to develop, operate and maintain information systems to support the business. If it is, information has a high impact. The impact of IT on the company is low if IT development is not one of the top three agenda items.

Determining which quartile of the grid a company is in is an important first step towards managing IT. Strategic companies are those where the impact and dependence are both high; for example, in the airline industry IT is so strategic that IT directors often sit on the main board of directors. Turnaround companies are those in industries where IT is changing the rules of the game; for example, the European insurance industry. Some companies, however, simply manage IT as a factory, taking advantage of its operating power to calculate huge volumes of data, but not considering IT as imperative to generate future advantages; for example, credit card processing. Support companies have a low dependence on information processing and IT is not considered vital to the business; for example, operating a zoo or plumbing.

McFarlan has devised six key questions to determine if IT is strategic (the bottom right quarter of the grid) to the firm:

(1) Are there ways to use the technology to create defensible entry barriers; for example, to produce economies of scale that competitors cannot match?
(2) Is there an opportunity to increase switching costs, increasing customer reliance on the systems; for example, airline Frequent Flier programmes?
(3) Are there opportunities to change the ground rules of competition?
(4) Can IT change competition from cost-based (that is commodity) competition to competition based on sustainable product differentiation?
(5) Can management use IT to build links to suppliers?
(6) Are there ways to use the technology as a product; for example, repackaging and sale of data files? (McFarlan and Warren, 1984).

By considering these questions and the ways an industry relates to information, managers can begin to change the way their companies use information for competitive advantage.

Investment in IT

When business leaders leaders gather to discuss the top issues in business IT, one inevitably emerges: how to extract the maximum value from the investment.

Investment in IT is significant, with figures ranging from two to five per cent of total revenue not uncommon. Evidence suggests that top companies spend more on IT than their competitors with figures ranging from three per cent to over nine per cent of turnover, depending on the industry (Figure 2.3) (Norton, 1988). Whatever the investment, managing the business IT effort effectively creates benefits that are captured periodically throughout the life of the commercial strategy and the system.

To make the most of any IT investment, the way the investment is integrated with the organization is of paramount importance. Table 2.1 shows the results of a survey by D. J. Silk on the impact of IT on UK organizations. The survey shows that business managers' first concern is the impact of IT on the organization. To get value out of the investment they want to understand the organizational dynamics involved. Second, the 'need for an information strategy linked to the business strategy' is important to link the business and IT objectives. Their third concern, security, points to the unknown variable in the IT/business equation. Business managers need to identify the exposure of the business to risks relating to breaches in information security arising from either accident or intent.

Table 2.1   Survey of information systems (IS): concerns of business managers. (*Source:* Silk, D. J. (1990): Current Issues in Information Management – Update. *International Journal of Information Management*, **10**, 178–81.)

(1)	Impact of IS on users; training
(2)	Need for an IS strategy
(3)	Security of information; hackers; staff security
(4)	Managing the IS function and IS development
(5)	Justifying the cost of new systems
(6)	Defining the requirements adequately
(7)	Changing data into useful management information
(8)	Back-up for vital systems; reliability
(9)	Integrating data; integration of databases
(10)	Ensuring systems meet managers' requirements
(11)	Standards; flexibility; being locked-in
(12)	Keeping informed about IT developments
(13)	Involvement of senior managers; political factors
(14)	Problem of updating large systems
(15)	Judging when to get into new technology
(16)	Attitude of IT professionals
(17)	Complying with legal and audit requirements
(18)	Distraction of staff by PCs
(19)	Assessing expert system
(20)	Getting tangible business advantage from IS

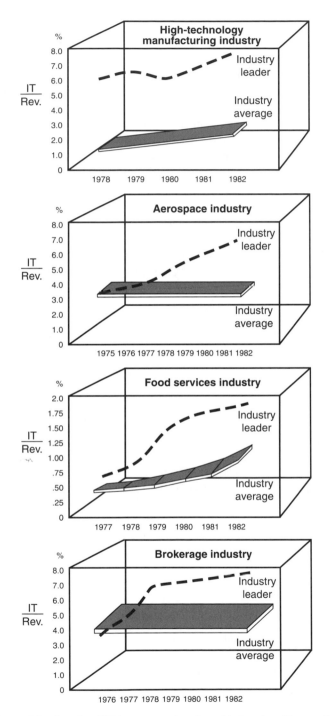

Figure 2.3   Levels of IT investment in selected industries. (*Source:* Nolan, Norton & Co.)

The impact of IT on the business can be difficult to predict or track. One major problem in managing business IT stems from the fact that most managers today are function-oriented. Managers are essentially specialists in their own areas: marketers understand marketing, financial people understand finance. The strategic benefits of IT, however, are often process-related, running across functions. For example, by making customer service information available to product designers, companies can more accurately design products to anticipate their customers' desires. Bruno Zuccharo, director of IT at Benetton, believed that: 'Functions must change with IT. Managers feel they understand IT, but they need to know much more about the opportunities. They need to know more about how to manage, use and involve people in IT and apply it across the business.' Managers can expand the scope of their functions by managing IT effectively and taking a cross-functional or process approach.

The effective management of IT also involves understanding its long-term implications and managers must perceive the investment as an integration of business purpose, technological capability and organizational learning. As the rest of this report examines in more depth, an effective business must consider these issues together.

Understanding the dynamics of the relationship between business purpose and IT is important in the formulation and targeting of a company's strategic intent. The impact of the enabling characteristics of IT, such as increasing the ease and presence of communication, supporting decisions with accurate data and improving the speed of transactions, is limited to the extent the management of the company uses these capabilities to improve its business efforts.

As Vic Mutnick, corporate vice-president of the New York Life Insurance Company, expressed it:

> Executives and managers need to realize that certain business practices just are not possible without IT. At New York Life, we considered what our business objectives were in concert with looking at what our technology could provide. We are able to do things we were not able to do before. For example, NYL can provide up-to-the-day pricing in stock funds and empower sales people in the field to have access to back office information from the field and underwrite insurance applications immediately. These are very real, fundamental changes to the way we operate that give NYL people an advantage.

The potential exists to change the way work is managed on a daily basis. The impact on work design is determined by the information content of the processes themselves. Although not all areas of information management can be improved with technology, many can, and the management imperative is to explore the opportunity for all business processes.

Action checklist

(1)   Does the business have IT links to customers or suppliers? Who benefits here?

(2)   What would happen if the information vital to your business disappeared? How long would recovery take? Could you carry on operations?

(3)   Is the industry undergoing any shifts in the competitive rules that suggest a role for management information?

(4)   What is management's attitude to the level of investment in IT in the business? Are results and benefits linked to investment levels clearly articulated so that management understands the interplay of IT and the business?

References

Abrahams, P. (1990). A place for everything and everything in its place. *Financial Times*, 10, 8 August

Bradshaw, D. (1990). Building blocks of efficiency. *Financial Times*, 14, 30 August

Cookson, C. (1990). A good fit on the factory floor. *Financial Times*, 15, 6 June

Cookson, C. (1990). On the road to a smoother ride. *Financial Times*, 18, 11 July

Griffiths, J. (1990). Fizz on the shop floor. *Financial Times*, 37, 22 May

Holberton, S. (1990). How BA tries to make friends and keep them. *Financial Times*, 16, 14 September

Hopper, M. D. (1990). Rattling SABRE – new ways to compete on information. *Harvard Business Review*, 118–25, May–June

Labich, K. (1990). The computer network that keeps American flying. *Fortune*, 44, 24 September

McFarlan, F. W. (1984). Information technology changes the way you compete. *Harvard Business Review*, 98–103, May–June. In addition to Professor McFarlan's articles, Harvard Business School has created a videotape on the Management of Information Technology which addresses many key issues. The notebook which goes along with the videotape provides helpful questions for managers such as these

Norton, D. P. (1988). The economics of computing in the advanced stages. *Stage by Stage*. Massachusetts: Nolan, Norton & Co.

Porter, M. E. and Millar, V. E. (1985). How information gives you competitive advantage. *Harvard Business Review*, 149–60, July–August

Stalk, G. Jr. (1988). Time – the next source of competitive advantage. *Harvard Business Review*, 41–51, July–August

Tilley, L. (1990). Tickets to ride on a full flight. *Financial Times*, 25, 16 August

3

Delivering the information

- An information system (IS) is a means of delivering information from one person to another. Information technology (IT) is the technical apparatus for doing so.

- Information systems rely on formal and informal sources; computers can only deal with formal sources of data, but can sort and reorder them in a useful way. IT is therefore not only actual machinery but also a resource which can closely integrate with informal information processes.

- A graphic representation of the structure and processes within a company is a useful way of analysing IT requirements.

- IT investments should also be evaluated on six counts: currency, content, quality, flexibility, importance and scalability by both managers and IT specialists.

- Information architecture is a second form of modelling, which captures the dynamics of the IT process.

- An information architecture comprises three types of information map: a data map; a network and communications map; and a technology map.

- Despite the sophistication of the modelling techniques, there are significant problems in extending a system devised for one country or organization to another. The needs of all users must be considered simultaneously, not sequentially.

Business managers develop frameworks, vocabulary and tools to describe how to make businesses more effective. As seen in Chapter 2, Michael Porter provides tools for managers to think about business strategy. Similarly, there are models that can be used to describe IT in the business. This chapter explores the distinction between 'information systems' and 'information technology'. It is a subtle distinction that helps to clarify management thinking. The chapter then shows how building a model of the business can provide a backdrop to analyse how its IT is functioning. Two types of model are described. The first is one that managers can build to show how information is currently used in the business; the second is a way to play for future information flows in the business.

Information systems and IT

When a business manager was asked recently to define 'information systems' his answer was typical: 'A method to deliver and transform raw data into information in a form we can use'. As enthusiastic as managers may be to use IT, it is important to remember that technology is not a requirement for an information system. An information system is a method of delivering information from one person to another. IT is the technological apparatus that conveys the information.

Information systems carry messages through channels with varying bandwidths. Tablets of clay were information systems, albeit with a very narrow bandwidth. Even in these days of modern management some very sophisticated information systems have been used without sophisticated technology; for example, just-in-time manufacturing for many years operated on a manual, hand-written card system. The 'T' in 'IT' is a mark of our civilization.

Information about the real world in business comes from many sources: from tomes which describe corporate policy and procedures; from talking with an authority who knows or appears to know; or from experience. Managers find out what they need to know about the real world by keeping an ear to the ground, asking a subordinate to carry out fact-finding missions or consulting their own memories (see Figure 3.1) (Land, 1990).

Formal and informal systems

Information systems can broadly be divided into two categories: formal, such as the policy and procedures book; and informal, such as conversations in the parking lot, wine bars or hallways.

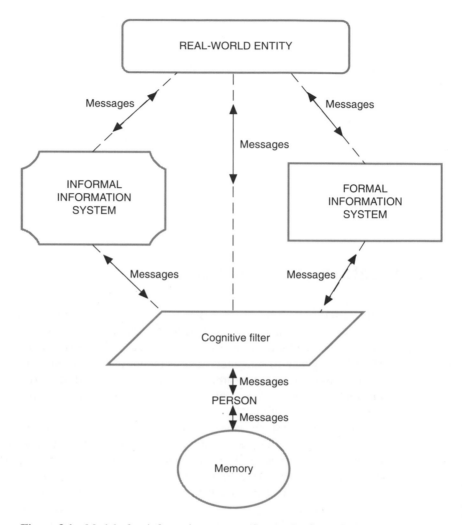

Figure 3.1   Model of an information system. (*Source:* Professor Frank Land, London Business School.)

Formal information systems provide descriptive information, mapping the real world into systems. Questions about such things as production quantity, statistical observations of quality and what the variances are between forecast and actual budgets can all be answered by formal information systems. However, the question of why there is a variance is very often qualitative or subjective. The variance may be because a different ordering of jobs was scheduled, but it may also include interpretive information outside the formal system, such as the fact that the salesman responsible for the budgets has a drinking problem. Professor Frank Land of London Business School explained:

> Business managers rely on a combination of information sources in both formal and informal networks. Until recently computer systems could only deal with formalized data. There was a rigid barrier in the application of IT between the formal and the informal, and systems designers used to adhere to this barrier.
>
> The problem with formal systems is that they are limited. The moment a formal information system is implemented, entropy occurs. The value of the information begins to decay almost from the moment the IT is introduced because the real world changes. To be effective a formal system would have to be capable of responding to such changes, which are not easy to codify. If managers receive inaccurate information from the formal systems they bypass them. After a time, as changes increase, the formal information system may become less relevant. There are many stories about managers receiving data about factory operations believing them to be accurate, while the factory was run by people in a completely different way.

The difficulty is one of timing, of synchronization. The computer is designed to receive and send messages between the real world and the person who uses it. Most of the formal systems are, if the Pareto rule is followed, only 80% accurate. Yet the 20% which is not received may represent an intolerable risk. The synchronization problem had to be solved.

Integrating the two systems

> As their cognitive filters – their set of ideas, beliefs and values – operate in the association between messages from outside sources and what they already know, managers adapt their knowledge. The information systems that managers actually use have an *ad hoc* quality and must change flexibly with informal information.
>
> In a comparison between computers and people, it could be said that people are flexible while computers are relatively inflexible. People tend to forget, however, whereas the computer can hold its finite memory intact. Human memory is uncertain, vital, culturally determined and, for most of us, imperfect. People have a sense of creativity, whereas computers are consistent, behaving in prescribed ways, and follow rules; people flaunt rules. People are capable of learning, whereas computers can basically perform three tricks: add 1, match things, and do it again. Computers build complex skills on the basis of these three abilities, yet they are limited in their capacity to learn. People are intuitive and have values, whereas computer systems embody the developers' values; the machine itself is valueless.

It is important that the two systems, formal and informal, relate to each other. IT is moving into the realm of informal communications. Advanced systems now tend not to be designed to execute a certain function but to offer a capability to be used by business managers. Electronic mail systems (Email) are an example of a capability. The format of the communication is left to the person, while the capability to pass messages over distance remains the domain of the machine. Within months of installing Email, companies experience a rapid increase in informal as well as formal communications.

Business managers have to try to harmonize the human side of information systems with the machine; this is the challenge of managing IT. They can have a mix of systems, some designed formally to report descriptive data and some as part of the infrastructure to support the informal communication processes. Ultimately they need to integrate their channels of communication to heighten their capacity to use information appropriately.

The two definitions of IT

The difference between information and data is that information is data in a usable form. Managers can make decisions and take action with information. It tells them something they did not know, hence it supplies added value and often contains a surprise element. If data relates something already known, it has no additional value.

IT can provide facilities to decode or reorder what a manager already knows in a useful, meaningful way. Knowledge differs from information in that knowledge has value and increases a person's capability over time. For example, understanding the principles of IT can help managers to create new ways of doing business.

There are, therefore, two definitions of IT. The first, the intensive definition, is limited to the hardware and software of computers. It relates to the physical characteristics of IT, such as electronic, digital, telecommunications, printers, processors, screens and so on. The second, the extensive definition, concerns what the equipment is used for. IT is the application of technology to business processes, gathering data and creating information that is valuable to managers who make business decisions. IT translates symbols into a usable form. IT, then, is a capability or a process not bounded by the immediate definition of the boxes and switches, but a challenge to managers with insight.

Building a business model

Managers control and coordinate, and the way they do this has an effect on both the shape of the organization and how information will flow in the business. In 1965 Robert Anthony of the Harvard Business School suggested that companies have control systems based on a three-tiered hierarchy: for planning, management and operations (Anthony, 1965). In the 1980s Henry Mintzberg, a leading scholar of organization design, offered an alternative view, consisting of forms of management structures that differ on the basis of how work is coordinated in the company (Mintzberg, 1983; Hampden Turner, 1990). Others suggest that as the information age reaches maturity, the middle management ranks will grow as operational tasks are computerized, senior executives will take on greater responsibilities, and the resulting form will look something like a diamond.

Whatever view is taken, the management of business is dependent on the management of business information throughout the business processes. Multidirectional information flows within business activities exist that must be managed. All these models have in common an effort to form units of people to carry out various processes. Some are functionally oriented, while others emphasize the cross-functional orientations. All are concerned with carrying out operations smoothly, with an optimal process flow. Figure 3.2 depicts Anthony's model of organizations, the major activity categories and the major process flows.

Balancing control and coordination

The management challenge of IT is to manage information effectively by balancing management control with management coordination, participation and leadership, whatever organizational form business takes on. For the business manager this means participating in both the leadership of the design of systems and in the technical development. For the IT manager this means leading the technical aspects of the IT effort while participating strongly in the development of business systems. Ultimate responsibility lies across the management functions because the management of IT is the management of information flow across processes. Coordination and control of business IT requires cooperation. Dr John Spackman, Director of Computing and Information Services at British Telecom, addressed this issue in Management View 3.

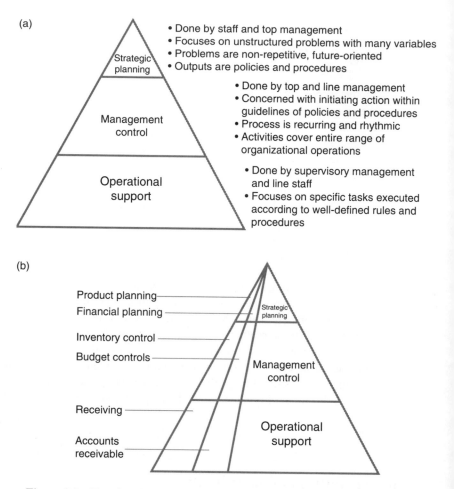

Figure 3.2   Functional model representation (a) A triangle showing the business separated by levels of decisions and the characteristics of these processes; (b) The same triangle showing the business functions on each level. (*Source:* Nolan, Norton & Co.)

Management View 3

Dr John W. C. Spackman, Director of Computing and Information Services, British Telecom

Business and technology managers must be hybrid managers, each understanding the other's areas. Future business success depends on it. Only managers with hybrid capabilities will be able to spot the opportunities resulting from

continues

continued

new ways of managing information and creating the greatest return on integrated corporate goals, utilizing both technology and human capabilities. For
the immediate future, we need a skilled workforce that is trained and adaptable.

At British Telecom we place a high priority on IT supporting customer
services. I coordinate systems-development operations and international communications, and I sit on the board. Our group-wide international and customer
service telecomms network receives a great deal of management attention.

Today we are competing in a changing world. The management trick
is to manage in a constantly changing environment. The efficient solution
of today is almost always a constraint for the future. So we build a high
level business model of today and then we change it to fit what we want for
tomorrow. Business analysis teams work with business managers who are
experts on the business processes. Value for money is important, so user
ownership is vital. We build a community of business interests and analysis.
Business managers define the standard of facilities.

We have built an infrastructure to share costs, but a lot of our applications are independent. Our main strategic aims are to have an integrated information network, such that information is a shared business resource. We have
structured a consistent architecture with application independence to accommodate the different ways to manage information; for example, managing
from the customer view, the financial view and transaction processing. In this
way BT copes with a great deal of complexity.

Business managers of tomorrow must manage change. For information
systems this means changing the systems with the changing business processes.
Execution is key, since more plans fail in execution than on the drawing board.

Developing the model

To be able to cooperate, business and IT managers need to develop a common
language to discuss how IT operates in the business. Building a business model
for the company like that shown in Figure 3.2 is useful to show the business
processes and to map the IT systems to the processes, so that everyone involved
can reach agreement about what is being done and what needs to be done to
fulfil the business purpose.

Building a picture of the fundamental structure of a company is an initial
way to represent graphically how IT is placed within the business. It helps
managers think about the key issues of structure and communication and how
they help or hinder the business process. The model will change as management's understanding of information, communication and how and who makes
decisions are worked through.

Real business models rarely conform to the exact triangle shape. The
triangle represents more activities in the operational area of the business than
in the management or strategic areas. Not all firms, however, operate in this

manner. Some companies have larger management than operational structures. For example, in industries where the knowledge content of jobs is high, such as publishing, there are more workers managing their own work than running the printing presses. This organizational form would look more like a diamond than a triangle. Thus business models vary according to the content of the work.

Level	Attempted coverage	Effective coverage	Effective Stage II	Stage III
Strategic			9	16
Management control	38	27	29	41
Operational support	57	40	41	55
Overall	46	32	34	46

A R&D
B Engineering
C Manufacturing
D Marketing
E Controller
F Personnel
G Legal

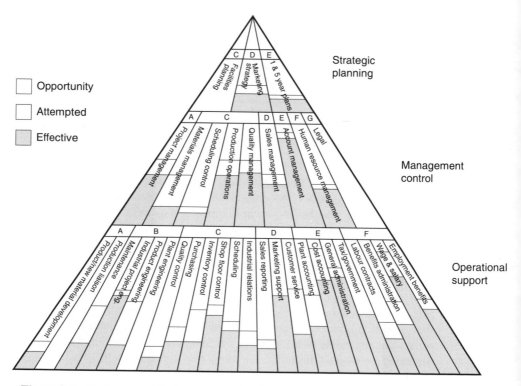

Figure 3.3 Business model of a company showing level of IT implementation. (*Source:* Nolan, Norton & Co.)

The company's activities can be classified into a set of processes or functions. For example, in a major financial service provider, the functions could be product development, marketing, sales, finance and administration, production, delivery and customer service. The major processes might be satisfying the customer, providing high quality products and services, and identifying niche opportunities. Figure 3.3 is one illustration of the major business functional areas.

After the major functions have been identified, management should then describe which major activities take place in each function in order to meet the requirements of the major business processes in the firm. Enough detail should be given to make the model useful.

Managers should then ask whether there are IT systems covering all or part of the functions. Describing what coverage there is involves looking at the business function, deciding whether IT is capable of assisting or replacing any of the processes, and to what extent it already does so. Figure 3.3 is an example of how the triangle of Figure 3.2 can be developed into a full model of IT usage in a company. It gives management a graphic summary of the status of IT in the business.

Using a model to plan IT investment

Looking at Figure 3.3, two types of information flow imbalances in this company become clear. There is a significant amount of operational coverage of systems, combined with some strategic support, yet a lack of management information systems. If this were a retail firm it could mean that sales information is provided in detail from shops, and that there is significant planning at the strategic level about what revenue is expected to be, yet it is difficult to aggregate the types and locations of sales. The plethora of data at the operational level therefore has little overall business value and cannot inform the strategy formulation level.

Management can easily be left out of the decision process if relevant information is not available or aggregated to be readily usable. Piles of operational reports that do not help the manager make decisions can land on desks, interrupting the flow of business rather than facilitating it.

The second type of information flow imbalance shown in this diagram is that of facilitating cross-functional processes. If the functions are not equally automated, information gaps can occur that impede business activities. For example, if customer service depends on information from marketing, manufacturing and delivery, the levels of automation need to be equivalent to facilitate an aggregated view of how customer service is taking place at any given time.

By 'walking through' the processes of the business on the business model, management can identify interdependencies in the process flows. Bottlenecks and contingencies can be planned for. The result is a model which shows how IT is currently used in a company. The graphic presentation makes it much easier to spot problems and opportunities.

Building such a model also helps management to prioritize investments. Business area requests for IT can be considered in the light of the overall IT investment. Requests for IT can seem like unrelated lists of projects. However, linking the requests to the needs indicated on the business model can help management plan programmes of investment that will satisfy broader business objectives. For example, a retail grocery company built a sales system linked to an order processing system to provide inventory supervision. It also provided valuable information that helped management to choose optimal delivery routes. The sales and order processing systems considered in conjunction helped to move each ahead in the queue of waiting projects, and provided management with an overall view of the value of implementing these systems before others.

Evaluating IT investment

IT is expensive, and its value to the company should be additionally checked by asking both business users and technical people how well IT integrates or fulfils their requirements. To do this the criteria below should be used, but determining the quality of the systems will always be a subjective exercise for the company in the final analysis.

Business managers should rate IT systems on the following six-factor list:

- *Currency.* The information available is up-to-date and the data are accessible and reliable.
- *Content.* This refers to the accuracy of the data.
- *Quality.* This term must be defined in context. Quality considerations are concerned with the degree to which the system helps the manager to do his or her job well or, alternatively, inhibits the business process.
- *Flexibility.* The ease of use of the system, the ability to generate changes or *ad hoc* requests, and the business manager's involvement in the systems process.
- *Importance.* The dependence of the business on the system and the level of security required.
- *Scalability.* A judgement of how the system will serve future business needs.

For IT managers the six-factor list includes many of the above considerations with the addition of technical performance criteria. For example, under currency the technology manager might add: transaction and response time; processing mode (mainframe, micro, etc.); terminal type (dumb, pc, workstation); data storage technique (tape, disk, etc.); and communications mode (slow, fast, hyperspace). Content would include complexity of the logic of the system and the language it is written in. Quality would include the systems facility for maintenance changes; ease of operation; number and kind of outages; and other problems such as operations requirements, quality controls and validation, ability to meet user requirements with user involvement and adherence to

standards. Flexibility would additionally refer to ease of use of the user interfaces, such as graphical representation structure; the modularity of the programs
that facilitate improvement; logical processing flow; responsiveness of the vendors; and the capacity for integration. Importance would include frequency of
operation and reliance of the related systems. Scalability would include the
expected life of the technologies *vis-à-vis* the growth prospects of the company.

By asking both business and technology managers about the coverage that
systems give to the functions and processes of the business, companies can
compare ratings to get an overall picture of their systems (see Figure 3.4).

Business manager view

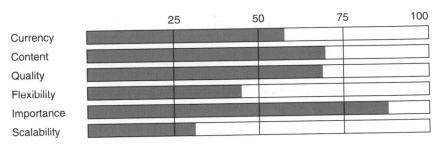

IT manager view

Combined quality assessment

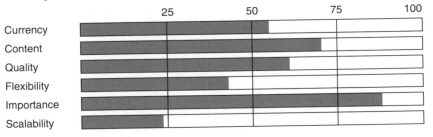

Overall quality index 58.75

Figure 3.4 Assessing business information system quality.

By combining the rating of the systems and the coverage depicted on the business model, management can now discuss the state of business IT in their company.

It is particularly important to take stock of the balance between the demand for IT involvement in the business processes and the ability of the company to supply. For example, if there is a huge systems backlog, then demand is outweighing supply. If there are idle IT resources, then supply is outweighing demand. Looking at the system's general coverage gives management an idea of where key developments can and need to take place to add to the power of the overall system portfolio.

Information maps and information architecture

The business models so far described give a snapshot of a company's IT investment at a particular moment in time, much as a balance sheet describes a company's financial position. Another type of model is required to capture the way information flows throughout the business. These models represent the information architecture of the business. they show where information is needed and by whom; what information is needed and how it will be used; how the information will travel throughout the business; and how the information will be managed from a technological and human resource point of view.

Information architecture

An information architecture is a set of models and plans that represents the flow of information throughout the business. Similar to the drawings an architect uses for buildings, the information architecture drawings are used by business and information technology managers to discuss information structures and facilities. The architectural representations indicate where information is created, used and can be updated. The hardware and software used to convey the information can be overlaid on to the information flow to indicate by what means the information will be conveyed. Communications plans show how networks will be put into place to ensure rapid and secure transportation of information. Above all, the information architecture allows business and IT managers to understand the dynamics of information, technology and business information needs by looking at a graphical representation of the dimensions of business information delivery: information, hardware and software, and communications.

The word 'structure' here does not imply rigidity; quite the opposite, in fact. An information architecture is a dynamic set of maps that track the interaction of the various factors. These are business processes, data, communications and technology resources. Philip Langsdale, director of planning at Midland Bank, described the flexibility required in an information architecture in Management View 4. These information maps must change with the needs of the business and, while charting current processes, allow the widest range of future options.

No information architecture attempts to map all of the information a business uses. For example, many of the informal flows of information that managers use (a random variety formed from newspapers, magazines, closed meetings and so on) cannot all be planned for within an architecture. However, the main information flows, the substance of management reports needed to plan and keep the business running and regularly used information used to plot the strategy of the company (that is customer, competitor, economic environment information), are readily identifiable and are represented in the architecture.

Creating a framework and developing the architecture

To begin to build an information architecture map it must first be clear what the business vision is; where the business is going; and where the business is today. These plans should have been captured in the model described earlier in this chapter.

The business information architecture fills in the details of who will be involved in the process, what their roles will be and how they will interact. It is important to keep the different types of models distinct. The business model shows how the existing systems cover the business functions and processes. The business vision and strategic initiatives describe a set of programmes to integrate business and IT plans. The business information architecture is a set of maps to use during the IT implementation.

Management View 4
Philip Langsdale, Director of Planning, Midland Bank

Business and IT managers need to ensure that they are getting a good return on IT investments. This means that IT investments should be made in as flexible a way as possible. Managers should not close business avenues by

continues

continued

structuring their IT systems in a way that closes off options. They might later regret their investment in inflexible IT.

Some companies are fiercely committed to designing systems like pouring concrete. The danger is that companies should not design systems to such an extent that business change is not possible. I am constantly amazed at financial services companies, for example, that forget that they may be divesting themselves of or changing in a radical way parts of their business. They should think about allowing for business options in the design of systems by, for example, systems modularization.

Information architecture helps managers know how to manage IT within a changing business. Most business people confuse what information they need with how it should be managed. The focus of the information architecture should be on setting out what business people need. It's up to the business people to decide to work with the IT people. We're pushing this hard at Midland. Line business executives need to know what information is available and how that information is managed. They don't need to know how the technology itself is managed. In this sense, the business information architecture and the business technology architecture should be differentiated.

The information architecture must be relevant to current business problems, to allow management to be capable of managing urgent situations within the business vision. At the same time we must understand the impact of information systems on the long-term future of the business.

Building an information architecture to support the business requires the creation of business programmes of change which allow better management of information. A programme is a set of projects, some related, which together effect change; for example, a new product development requires efforts in marketing, training, IT, and so on. In this way business managers need not be bewitched by new technology, but can put it to work to gain advantage.

They can also use what they have to gain advantage. There is a tendency for some managers always to look towards the new IT rather than think about new ways to get value from what the business already has. The bulk of IT work actually goes into utility systems, the platforms that make all the ventures possible. Managers can use infrastructure already established to achieve the vision quickly and cheaply.

Business people must work with systems people on the IT architecture. Throughout the structure of projects the roles and responsibilities of business and IT managers must be clear. The role of the project owner is a business management responsibility because it concerns what the business does, how he or she manages the business. When investment in IT runs to the size of our budget (£407m per annum), performance control over information has to become a shared responsibility between business and IT managers. In that way we can get our arms around the value of IT and create the maximum return.

If the vision and strategy are determined, the second step is to identify clusters of business activity. A cluster of business activity is a group of business processes that logically fit together to form a coherent group. For example, in an insurance company a cluster might be formed to represent customer sales and service efforts (see Figure 3.5). In this company, Insurco, the field agents meet the customers in their homes to discuss policy sales. The field agent has a portable microcomputer that helps him or her to demonstrate the available products to the customer and to change the products to suit the customer's changing assessments of what he or she would like to buy. A key selling point in insurance is to be able to modify the policy offering in the home of the customer during the selling process since, as the customer considers future needs with the help of the agent, new considerations may come to light.

During the sales call the field agent communicates with the regional marketing department's product development database to peruse the product and service offerings. The customer then happens to mention that a claim that they expected to be processed has not come through. The field agent accesses the claims department database at the claims office to check the status of the claim. The customer also mentions that the amount of investment in their

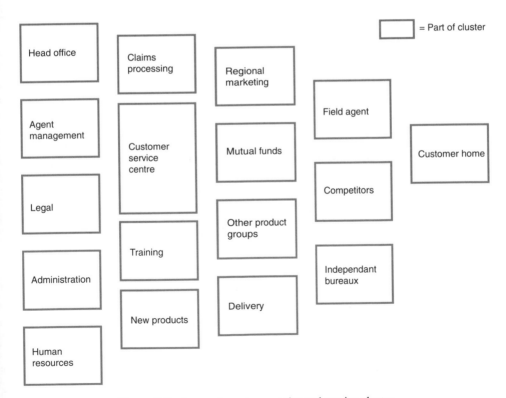

Figure 3.5   Insurco's customer sales and service cluster.

mutual funds account with Insurco has a bearing on their decision on how much to spend on an insurance policy. The field agent calls up the customer portfolio to look at the current status of all accounts. In addition the field agent recalls that there is a new ruling from head office on issuing policies to mutual funds holders. He or she accesses the ruling on the portfolio database at head office.

In the process of this simple exercise to sell a policy to a customer, the information needs of the field agent can become quite complex. The capability to access information to look at Insurco's product and service portfolio, the current status of claims processing or work in progress, the current value of mutual funds accounts (that is the relationship of the customer with Insurco as currently reflected in the customer portfolio) and the current ruling on policy and procedures from head office must be made available to the field agent to help him or her close the sale.

Clusters differ from company to company depending on management's views on how the processes should be clustered to carry out their business. No two businesses are ever alike, although companies within the same industry may bear some resemblance to one another. Because the business information architecture depends on how management structure their business, it is always unique.

The business information architecture consists of three maps:

- A data map that shows what information is needed where and by whom.
- A network and communications map that shows the flows of information.
- A technology map that indicates what technology, hardware and software, will be used to provide the information.

Data maps

Business is changing with the increasing availability of data communications which can provide a tremendous lift to the business, as the example of Insurco shows. This is confirmed by a strategy director in a major European firm: 'In earlier years possibilities to use IT were in the emergent phase due to the development of the technologies. Yet the possibilities were not practised as much as they can be now due to advancements made in data communications.'

Difficulties in synchronizing data might mean that an insurance company, for example, could have five separate listings for one customer just in terms of name and address. Providing one reliable source of information that is always accurate and up-to-date is a relatively new phenomenon in many businesses. Andrew Rigby, finance director of Chartham Paper Mills, remarks: 'The development of decision-making databases has improved dramatically over the past decade. For example, they can now configure summations of data in ways managers can interpret without having to wade through piles of rubbish to get to the salient point.'

Managers can increasingly rely on software to send data throughout the business and expect systems integration techniques to allow all sorts of

technologies to interconnect seamlessly. The data map identifies what information is needed where and by whom. To draw the map managers must ask the
people involved in the architecture process to build a data model. Data are the
pieces of information a company uses in the course of running its business.
Thus, in the example customer, field agent, product and so on are all examples
of key data necessary to the business.

Attributes are the characteristics of the key data; for example, the attributes for a customer would include name, address, preferences for products and
so on. The managers and operations people in the company must identify the
key data groups and their attributes. These are unique to a company because
they identify the major concepts around which the business operates. Figure
3.6 indicates some key data groups and attributes for Insurco.

Data maps can be built for all of a company's major processes. By keeping them current management can coordinate information needs more easily
and plan more effectively. Bottlenecks, such as the need for simultaneous and
synchronized data communication, become apparent (for example, the claims

Customer sales and service efforts

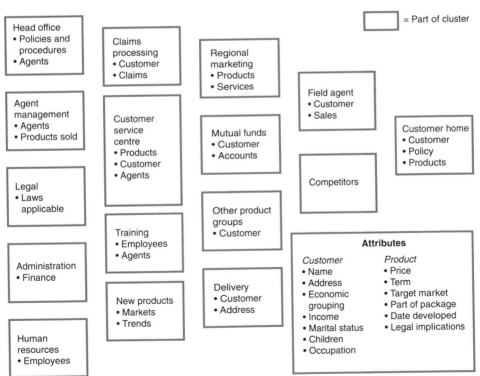

Figure 3.6   Insurco's data map. (Full data map would include more detailed groupings.)

processor and field agent needing access to the same file seemingly at the same time). Complexities in the interpretation of key data groups (such as naming all the relevant attributes that will give value to the business for a particular group, that is customer economic group for customer) can be sorted out.

Exploring data maps may also bring to light information available in the company that is not being used to great advantage. For example, the customer service area can be used to collect customer preference information which may not have been revealed to the field agent. If the customer service representative captures this information, the field agent may be able to close a sale more easily. For example, in Insurco the customer service centre answers various customer questions about products. During a recent survey Insurco found that customers like to find out about products without always having to refer to the field agent. However, if the field agent is then provided with that information, he or she can form a more definitive profile of the customer's desires that can help in the next sales call.

Networking and communications maps

The network and communication map of a company shows the flows of information. Figure 3.7 continues the example. For the field agent system to be effective, communications from the field to the various parts of the company must be effective. Tracing through the vital lines of communication from various stakeholders' points of view builds up management's understanding of the importance of various communication flows. In essence, the map indicates the interdependencies of the information flows.

Strategic initiative programmes often highlight the need for communications technology, in conjunction with the need to train managers to use communications and to be able to spot opportunities to form communication links. In the broadest sense, communications can mean any effort to convey information over distance with the maximum effectiveness.

Communications have been greatly facilitated by technical developments such as the switch from analog- to digital-based technology, including ISDN, which allows increased integration of networks and various media including text, voice and video; fibre optics, which allow fast communications at prices that most businesses will be able to afford; and imaging, which transforms business from paper-based to image-based communications. In Case Study 3.1 Thornton May, Director of Imaging Research at the Nolan, Norton Institute, described changes that have occurred at Bank of Boston as a result of introducing the use of imaging to the organization.

The regular 'bugbear' of telecommunications is that, to date, there are various standards and protocols existing for data, image and text transfer. These issues will be sorted out as countries realize to what extent their businesses rely on the electronic infrastructure to compete in world markets.

Customer sales and service efforts

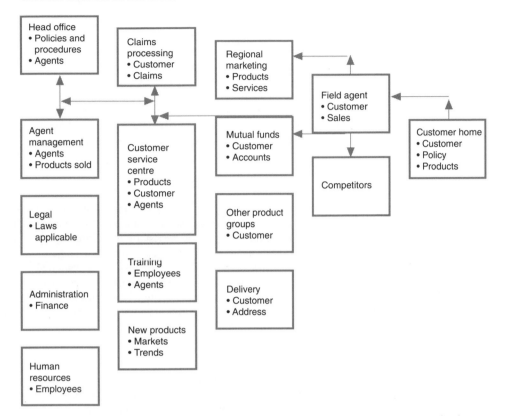

Figure 3.7   Insurco's network and communication map. (Full network and communications map would include more detailed groupings. This figure illustrates the flow for the information described in the text.)

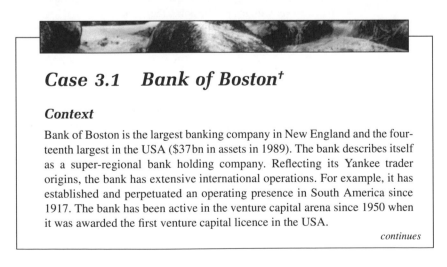

Case 3.1   Bank of Boston†

Context

Bank of Boston is the largest banking company in New England and the four-teenth largest in the USA ($37bn in assets in 1989). The bank describes itself as a super-regional bank holding company. Reflecting its Yankee trader origins, the bank has extensive international operations. For example, it has established and perpetuated an operating presence in South America since 1917. The bank has been active in the venture capital arena since 1950 when it was awarded the first venture capital licence in the USA.

continues

continued

The economic downturn in New England caused the bank to suffer a significant and continuing drop in profitability. It experienced a 78% decline in 1989 net income which fell to $70m from $322m in 1988. First quarter 1990 earnings were about 50% of those generated in the same period of 1989. The atmosphere at the bank certainly is not expansive with regard to approving expensive new technology initiatives.

The bank has five check-processing centres in New England running five different hardware/software configurations. 'This is a set-up with obvious cost and service inefficiencies,' says Dick Domingoes, senior manager in charge of document-processing technology.

Why change?

The bank seeks significantly to reduce net operating expenses. A data centre consolidation offers enormous potential for cost reduction. However, basing the consolidation on existing technology runs the risk of premature technological obsolescence. The consolidation initiative was conceived in conjunction with the introduction of imaging technology. Images can be captured quickly and then transmitted electronically to workstations, stored on magnetic or optical media and printed on advanced function laser printers. More than 50bn checks a year are written in the USA. Imaging can significantly reduce the costs associated with processing them.

Vision

Mike Lezinski, director of data processing and deposit management services, has embraced the organization's mission of customer service. The expensive imaging initiative was perpetuated in the face of declining profitability because the technology was thought to:

- improve customer service
- catalyse a rethinking of how work is done in the organization
- place power with the people doing the work
- establish a platform that will grow with the organization
- decrease costs in the long term.

What the bank did

Believing that image processing represented the inevitable end state of transaction processing and service-intensive financial products, the bank sought to create a homogeneous platform that could bring home the benefits of imaging on an enterprise basis. In sequential order it:

- re-examined the existing document-processing strategy
- rescanned the technological horizon
- entered into a partnership with the largest provider of technology
- embarked on a 22-month migration path to integrating the five data centres on a common image-enabled technology pattern.

continues

continued

Outcome and future

Customer service has improved. The knowledge workers at the Dorchester facility (the pilot site) played a significant role in resculpting their work environment. They designed workflows that reduced the headcount and established tremendous opportunities for job enrichment. The technology platform in place is one of the most advanced in the industry. It establishes a baseplate (with no more redundant hardware/software) into which all technology vendors, not just the bank's partner, can integrate. The facility is processing four million cheques a day.

Technology maps

'Technology is sometimes flavour of the month,' one distraught IT manager said. 'Business managers go off and order kit on the basis of one conversation with a friend without understanding how any of it fits.' This is a problem many companies encounter. Business managers seeking, perhaps quite rightly, a quick solution buy the first technology that looks promising. This can be described as a problem in search of any solution.

At the other end of the spectrum most large companies have one system that management continues to feed, although they have lost sight of what the original system was supposed to do. The system takes on a life of its own and the user sees nothing – there is no payback. This is what one firm calls the phenomenon of the 'runaway system'. New projects suffer because resources are tied to non-productive systems. IT jobs, felt to be at stake, get aligned to particular systems. In this case the IT people have too much power. It is a situation where the solution is in search of a problem.

There are clearly dangers in relying on either type of business information management myopia. The process requires two sets of eyes: the business manager's and the IT manager's. In the case of technology it is necessary for the two sets of managers to communicate well. Business managers must be able to understand the capability of the technologies, while IT managers must be able to communicate the capabilities to the business managers and understand the business processes.

Technology maps provide a common ground for discussing the realities, potentialities and constraints of given technologies. Vendors will often give a view about the capabilities of the technologies they offer that is not based on consideration of the particular business's requirements. Management need to undertake a level-setting exercise in terms of their expectations of the technology and a consideration of its potential.

Customer sales and service efforts

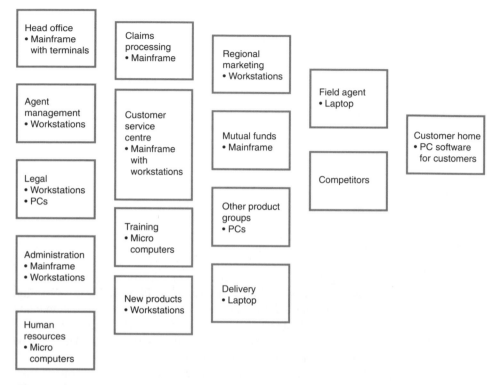

Figure 3.8   Insurco's technology map. (A full technology map would include more detail. This illustrates a high-level interpretation.)

The technology map will differ in detail for each business according to management style, type of industry and so on. As a minimum the technology map should include a breakdown of the major technologies covering the company's activities: that is, whether the process is supported by mainframe or micro technology and how the nodes of the networks interrelate (that is, the technological dependencies of the systems such as the dependence on a particular server to act as the 'traffic cop' for various departments). In essence, the technology map should include enough information for business managers to understand the major implications of the technology's constraints and opportunities for their business (see Figure 3.8). As business managers become better acquainted with technologies, more detailed maps can be drawn.

Using technology maps for competitive edge

Nissan has established a leading set of systems in its manufacturing plant at Sunderland in the UK, which is able to plan and monitor production to a high degree of flexibility. John Hope of Nissan Europe said:

> Nissan's achievements at Sunderland have been supported by a technology platform which is able to give rapid response. We use fourth generation technology, almost exclusively, and couple this with a development of methodology which delivers systems quickly. The IT advantage of being a young company, established in 1984, is that we use new technology to develop new systems. In fact, we developed systems in 1988 to replace totally the systems used to launch manufacturing in 1986.

Not every company has the 'advantage' of starting from scratch. Most companies have a portfolio of systems at varying degrees of age, currency in technology and relevance to the business. These issues can be brought out with the information architecture for management's consideration. Management need to know what the major information issues are in the business. Explicit partnerships between IT and business managers help to identify critical areas of the information fabric of the business.

Identifying which type of system is needed – utility, providing the infrastructure to the business; retail, providing specific applications for business process; and ventures, providing risky yet potentially rewarding new applications of IT – helps guide management in making investment decisions.

Together the data, network and communications, and technology maps identify what information needs to flow through the business activities via which media and systems. By determining the flow of information through these maps, management can identify opportunities and bottlenecks for the business's information flows. By graphically representing the data flows and the technology required to support them, managers can move on to implementation plans with detailed knowledge of what needs to be done in IT to accomplish the strategic objectives.

Developing a global information architecture: the fallacy of roll-out

Management can begin to develop a global information architecture by coming to terms with some key concepts and guidelines. The first of these, the fallacy of roll-out, refers to the most common pitfall companies find when beginning to build international information systems.

Contrary to popular belief, well-designed local systems are not necessarily readily transferable to other geographic locations. The experience of many companies confirms that designing systems without a global perspective, using traditional design methods, is tremendously costly. Not only are they extremely expensive to roll out around the world, but their functional quality also diminishes with each successive implementation.

Many US companies have developed a system at home, taken the 'core' of that system to another country and tried to implement it with 'minor changes'. US systems do not necessarily work in European countries, and vice versa. Global variations must be taken into account in the design phase of potential global systems, otherwise a situation exists in which the same set of shoes is being constantly stretched and shrunk to fit various sizes of feet.

One company's experience

In the mid-1970s a major European manufacturing company built an order-processing system in the UK and then decided to roll it out as a pan-European system. The second country in the 'phased implementation' process was France. The idea was that since there was already a system in the UK, why not capitalize on economies, use the 'core system' developed in the UK and ask France what it wanted to add on to that system. Most of the UK system had to have functional modules rewritten or bypassed in order to adapt it to French needs. The third country in the process was Germany. France relayed accounts of the difficulties of implementation and advised Germany to start with its revised version. Germany, hoping to capitalize on France's experience and in an effort to maintain company consistency, agreed. Germany then called for extensive modifications to add on or bypass the French modules that were designed to bypass the UK modules. The systems maintenance people soon developed long faces to match their long hours.

The point is that as the system went from country to country it had a cascading effect of lost functionality and quality. This is by no means a sequence of events limited to one company; it is a standard multinational approach to (and result of) systems development. The company measured the UK system's degree of effective coverage. The effective coverage in France was lower, and in Germany lower still. No wonder common systems get a bad name.

The next country in the process took a look at the experience of France and Germany and refused to be the next recipient of the phased implementation. It said the systems did not apply to its business. 'You do not understand, we are different,' translates into, 'I do not want to implement that system.' The ultimate aim was to involve 15 countries. The painful process took seven years.

By 1987 the company wanted to redesign and then connect these various systems. It called in external consultants to assist with the front end architectural design. As a first step they brought together cross-functional, cross-geographic managers to describe the various functional activities in their businesses. At the beginning, based on past experience, there was a general consensus that 20% of the systems could be the same and 80% would have to be different. The countries were adamant about this. The often repeated comment was: 'Forget building the intergalactic global system, what we need are basic local systems.' As a result separate business and data models were built for each country so that they could clearly understand the basics and opportunities.

Building the functional models enabled these managers to see that what they did was more similar than they had expected, even though various parts of the company were at different stages of development. The team eventually reached the conclusion that 80% of the systems was the same and 20% different. They then developed the blueprints or maps of the required software applications, data and communications, allowing for consistency and diversity. This set of maps defines the global consistency that they can put in systems allowing for 15 different variations.

Global architecture cannot be 100% the same

Companies cannot complete a 100% architecture. The purpose of the global architecture is to define what can be the same so that everything else can be different. It enables the company to make trade-offs that define the boundaries of global consistency and local look and feel. The first attempt at architecture will be minimal but incredibly powerful.

Similarly it may be a mistake to make a 'complete' data-flow model at the beginning. It may be too complex. The aim should be to develop the global architecture around the company's strategic initiatives, such as supporting a global customer, managing global employees or transferring global knowledge.

Many companies still insist on developing complete financial systems for each country and a worldwide chart of accounts. While no one would challenge the necessity of having accurate, timely financial information, the complete, consistent system approach may forever keep the company's resources tied up, leaving it unable to address more market-oriented programmes. By going after absolute homogeneity in financial systems the company may be pursuing global IT in an area that does not address its most urgent strategic needs.

An alternative would be to determine the significant business indicators needed on a global business level, and to build a database to pull out those figures. As Johnson and Kaplan (1987) say, entirely new management account-ing systems must be developed for new Information Age corporations. All the rules are changing. In terms of managing a business this means that systems must be designed around the processes of the business in dealing with cus-tomers, sources, products and distribution.

The development of a global architecture takes into account the diversity of functions, locations and data. The global architecture moves away from a geographic concept of doing business and focuses on the business concept and flow. By forcing individual sites to look at problems from multifunctional perspectives, businesses gain powerful capabilities to develop consistency while supporting local look and feel, which in turn enables the company to leverage resources and connect for global advantage.

Action checklist

(1)   What level of understanding about the technology do business managers in your company need to have? What level do they have?

(2)   Has your company carried out an assessment of information systems? How effective are the systems in place today? Will they support growth and future business plans?

(3)   What are the most important information flows in your business?

(4)   What are the major clusters of business activity?

(5)   What are the key data groups in your business?

(6)   What is the current state of the communications infrastructure in your company?

(7)   How does the company develop IT internationally? Do various perspectives from various areas contribute to the 'core systems'?

References

Anthony, R. (1965). *Planning and Control Systems, A Framework for Analysis.* Division of Research, Graduate School of Business Administration, Harvard University

Hampden Turner, C. (1990). Henry Mintzberg: A Profile. *Business Strategy Review,* Centre for Business Strategy, London Business School

Johnson, H. Thomas, Kaplan, Robert S. (1987). *Relevance Lost.* Boston, Massachusetts: Harvard Business Press

Land, F. (1990). Lecture given on 10 October at the London Business School

Mintzberg, Henry. (1983). *Structure in Fives: Designing Effective Organisations.* Prentice-Hall International Inc., New Jersey

† Prepared by Thornton May, director of imaging research at the Nolan, Norton Institute

4

IT for competitive advantage

- The way managers develop the information profile of a company can build competitive advantage.
- Every company has a series of critical events in which information availability is critical in delivering products and services to the market.
- Key business cycles are customer ordering, manufacturing production and delivery to distribution. By viewing the whole system as one business cycle, managers can ensure that information flows smoothly throughout the business.
- Five competitive objectives companies have that illustrate the importance of information management are: improving customer service, improving time to market, improving quality, improving management communication and increasing global reach.

Each industry uses IT differently

The description of what determines competitive advantage is a profile of the particular competence or hallmark a company has in the marketplace. By definition, no two companies have exactly the same competitive advantage. Similarly, companies have different profiles of how they use information. The flows, management and value of information determine the effect the use of information technology will have on competitive advantage. There are several fundamental strategic processes to which IT has the potential to contribute. Examples of these are: improving customer service, improving time to market, improving management communication, improving quality and increasing global reach. A company's information strategy plays a key role in differentiating the company in the marketplace.

Club Med is a company that is taking advantage of information to create competitive advantage. Club Med has a unique business information profile. The management team is looking to the future, searching for new ways to use information in relevant ways for the business, scanning the globe for important business information indicators that can contribute to Club Med's unique business information profile.

Gilbert Trigano, the company's chairman, discussed the future trends of the business and illustrates how timely information is increasingly important for companies in determining their precise, competitive advantage.

> The Asian market, with office openings in growing markets such as Taiwan, Korea, Malaysia and Singapore, are broadening our base. It is quite obvious that, of the three major markets, Europe, America and Asia, the latter is going to experience the fastest growth, proportionately, in the coming decade, although it won't match our largest market, Europe, or the American market, in the present decade.
>
> Clearly, too, based on present vacation consumption trends, we can expect to witness two apparently contradictory phenomena: on the one hand, people are taking two-to-four-day breaks to places close at hand, and on the other, longer stays in distant lands. We expect this phenomenon to spread to all of the industrialized countries. There is also a growing trend toward later and later bookings. Obviously, we are going to have to redefine our development strategy more precisely. Our management teams and the board are currently working on this.
>
> Broad trends are coming into sharper focus. Behind the diversity of consumer behaviour and changing tastes and means, two apparently contradictory trends are emerging. First, there is a strong trend toward an increasingly international clientele. This is clearly perceptible among young couples and single individuals who live in large cities, spend their lives in offices and flats, are exhausted by the stress of careers, commuting and the compartmentalization of their lives and who desire the spontaneity and self-discovery that our vacations afford. Second, a broad segment of customers wants to take a holiday in villages where everyone speaks the same language.
>
> In the corporate segment, corporations are turning to us for their conventions, seminars and incentive travel, but they also come to us to relax and mingle in a friendly, hierarchy-free atmosphere, where teams can be forged and fortified.

It is around these, and a few other lines of development, that Club Med is shaping its strategy, backed, fortunately, by a new Electronic Data Processing concept which will be fully operational this autumn, after five years of work and substantial investment.

Notice how Mr Trigano mentioned the importance of key consumption trends. As the company becomes a more global corporation, information about changing customer preferences has more value to Club Med. Being able to define customers' needs and wants more accurately permits the company to gauge its strategy more precisely. Case 4.1 describes the development of the new reservations system at Club Med. The system helps the company to track customer preferences closely and to develop new products targeted at growing markets.

The company is also developing multimedia point-of-sale stations, called 'Les Bornes Interactives'. These stand-alone sales and demonstration units have extended the idea of the automated teller machine (ATM). The multimedia stations will allow customers to examine holiday locations, play short videos demonstrating the sports and other activities at the locations, select a holiday and make a purchase. Tickets and written information confirming the holiday are sent directly to the customer's home. This invention makes it possible for Club Med to conduct business with a customer without having a sales office or personnel located at the multimedia station. It is possible, therefore, to position these stations in places where having a sales office would not be possible, but where there is a heavy traffic of customers, such as in busy shopping centres.

Case 4.1 Club Med

Context

Club Med operates 139 vacation villages in 35 countries and runs hotels, cruises, tours and leisure real-estate. In 1991, sales reached 7,841,939,000FF, with 8,064,200 hotel days filled for a 64.8% occupancy rate. Club Med is a brandname recognized worldwide.

Why change?

Tourism is an industry that is increasingly dealing internationally and hence with the diversity of worldwide customers. The company made the decision to build a state-of-the-art reservations booking system in real-time. The system objectives were to provide a centralized reservation system available 24 hours a day, seven days a week, 365 days a year to accommodate different market hours around the world.

continues

continued

Vision

As Serge Trigano, chief executive officer of Club Med describes the investment in IT for competitive advantage: 'We have invested in the concept of the holiday. Our customers believe that the holiday begins when they leave their homes and offices to go to the holiday location. The quality of their transportation, their arrival, everything affects what they think of us. We are building information systems so that we can integrate our information flows about the customer experience as the global tourism industry concentrates. We are leaders in the global tourism industry.'

Georges Vialle, director of information and telecommunications leads the IT effort at Club Med. 'The IT function is a strategic one. Our objective with the reservations system was to increase help to sales and marketing. We wanted to achieve product and price flexibility. The functionality we developed includes marketing, management of the distribution network, price, sales, connections with sub-contractors, product definitions and yield management. We have a network that connects the villages to the host so that information about arriving customers can be sent to the villages. When the value is seen by the customer, then we have a competitive advantage.'

Different industries will have different strategic information needs depending on the competitive environment. If an industry is competing on margins, rationalization of the industry will probably be occurring, and supplier linkages will be vitally important. If the industry has reached a stage where companies are competing on the differences of features of the products and services, then systems such as customer databases will be of primary importance. Making beneficial tradeoffs in strategic information management systems will depend on executives' and managers' abilities to read the competitive environment properly and to translate their information needs into actionable systems.

Information flows

To identify competitive information system needs accurately, executives and managers look at the key events that occur in the business process. Information that may be of competitive value is associated with these key events of the business. By tracking this information, management can more precisely decide on the actions to take. Their decisions will be based on the events and the business cycles affected by changes in both the competition and the marketplace.

Point of event

A point of event is a key trigger point in a business's activities, such as a customer's purchase, a shipment of goods or the delivery of a service. These events are critical to the company's performance. Jan Carlson, chief executive of Scandinavian Airline Systems (SAS), referred to any point of event that a customer is involved in as a 'moment of truth' for the company. Managing the customers' perceptions by focusing management attention on moments of truth is a technique SAS employs to ensure the high quality performance of their customer service.

Key points of events can be grouped in cycles. For example, a distribution cycle may consist of the event of finishing the goods on a production line, loading the goods on to transportation vehicles and delivering the goods to the customer. A product development cycle consists of the conception of the product, the illustration of the concept, the rendering of a prototype and the delivery of production specifications.

Points of event are associated with information of value to the organization. By focusing and identifying the key points of event in a business and defining the information of value about these events, managers build a set of performance measures and monitoring systems about the company's key business processes.

Tracking key cycles in the business

The importance of tracking key cycles in the business can be illustrated by the following example. There is a television advertisement for a fax machine. In it, a young businessman is waiting by a fax machine. He is waiting for one long fax to print slowly out. In other offices, several executives are trying to fax through orders to the company, but the line is busy. The young man's boss enters the fax room. 'Any business?' she asks. The young man says, 'Just one fax order.' Meanwhile the potential customers are fed up with waiting and call another supplier who owns several fax machines.

Customer ordering is a key cycle in the business that includes communication with the customer, the specification of the customer's needs, the specification of the suppliers' goods and services and the design, making and delivery of that product or service. Increasingly, managers are viewing functional cycles as part of the whole business cycle. For example, many companies would add a step in the cycle just described. That step would be to gather information about the customer's preferences that were or were not met in that one transaction, to keep the customer's description in the business system to enable the company to serve that customer again.

British Airways is in the middle of building a massive customer database to track customers' purchase patterns. The idea behind the project is that the definition of a customer should not be focused on one or two transactions, but that the customer is someone who makes several purchases over a lifetime. This extended view allows British Airways to keep working with the customer to design and develop products and services based on customer information. They have just recently launched a programme for first-class passengers that allows customers to alter the traditional service offered on long-haul flights. The first-class passenger will be able to choose whether they want to dine during the flight or ahead of time in the airline's lounge. They will also be offered a seat that is made up as a single bed that will allow them to sleep almost the entire length of the trip. This product offering was developed at the passengers' suggestions. Case 4.2 describes several initiatives the company is carrying out to capture competitive advantage to be the world's number one airline.

By identifying key business cycles and points of event in the business, companies can more closely shape their product and service offerings to the market demand. Key information management also occurs across functions to enable the business cycles to operate effectively and efficiently. By highlighting the internal performance measures required to meet customer requirements, internal management of processes support the information flow of the key cycles. On a wider basis, firms scan the external environment to capture and manage information that may affect their competitive position.

Case 4.2   British Airways

Context

British Airways is the world's largest international passenger airline. In 1992, the company carried 25 million passengers, made 261,000 flights and carried 500,000 tonnes of cargo. BA flies to 150 destinations, in 70 countries, with 230 aircraft.

Vision

The strategic direction of the company is to grow to be the world's leading airline. Growth will come from both organic growth and acquisition. Unlike other airlines, BA has decided against a diversification strategy and states clearly that the company's objective is 'to be the best and most successful company in the airline industry'. The mission of the information management team at British Airways is 'to achieve business advantage for British Airways through being the world leader in the application of airline information technology'.

continues

continued

What BA did

British Airways Business Systems (BABS) is the on-line worldwide reservations service that runs 24 hours a day, seven days a week, 365 days a year. Information available on BABS includes airline schedules for agents, seat availability, international fare systems, group bookings, car hire and hotel accommodation. Passenger bookings can be accessed by any terminal connected to the system anywhere in the world with the appropriate authority. Information includes routing, departure date, name, contact address, fare details and special requirements. The aim of the system is to process ticketing, departure control, passenger handling, load-control information, weather, flight, planning and fares.

At any given moment, BABS holds over two million passenger records, 100,000 of which change every day as a result of messages received at the rate of up to 200 per second from all over the world. The system supports the ability to quote some 40 million different fares. The real-time database is held on 238 IBM 3380 disks, each having 1.9 gigabytes of available storage. The mainframes are capable of performing 22 million instructions per second under the current operating system. All this information is copied at intervals on to backup security units.

Outcome and future

British Airways has had considerable success in developing systems as products to other airlines. These products are sold through Speedwing, a group established in 1990 to sell IT products and services. Speedwing sells a range of systems covering such areas as ground meteorology, aeronautical information, flight planning, reservation services, departure control and fares. In the past two years, revenue has almost doubled to over £50 million, and its customer list includes over 50 airlines.

Nick Marbrow, British Airways technical sales manager commented: 'From an airline's point of view, the reservation system is the airline's main vehicle for generating revenue. Our on-line transaction systems have helped British Airways make massive strides in terms of profitability. Our competitive edge lies in our ability to deliver good technology, closely aligned to our business needs, ahead of our competitors. In the future, we shall continue to develop the vision of airline technology so that we can provide these products and services to other companies.'

Information management in the business environment

In the energy industry, Elf Acquitaine, as one of the world's ten largest companies, monitors and scans an enormous amount of competitive, economic and political information to inform managers about conditions that may affect the performance of the company. The company's major activities include oil and gas, chemicals and pharmaceuticals. Since the company operates on a worldwide basis with oil and gas reserves as well as markets located in various corners of the world, the company needs extensive information systems to track global activities. Breakthroughs in research in both the chemical and pharmaceutical businesses can occur in many places. Changes to economic conditions in one area of the world can influence other geographies to a great extent. Information management needs access to global information on a real-time basis, but also needs to be kept informed about macro and micro economic forces that might affect the company.

Making information available to managers around the world is a massive effort on which the company spends millions each year. Jacques Moulin, corporate information manager, described the scanning activities: 'Our job is to add value to information coming into the company from outside. We receive information from a wide variety of sources covering economic, political and market conditions. Of course, this is too much information for business managers to digest, so we have to select what information goes to whom and when. The availability of accurate, timely information on a global basis is still somewhat rare, although there are a few sources. So we have to gather a lot of the information ourselves.'

As companies become more global, world market conditions will be more closely connected. The need for world information sources will grow tremendously well into the next century. To date, most companies without vast resources for environmental scanning must rely on local market indicators and determine from these, on an aggregate basis, how different conditions will affect their companies. However, recent events such as wars and economic strikes that have taken a toll on a wider range of companies, illustrate how events in one part of the globe can drastically affect business in others.

Value of information

Information only has value if it is timely, accurate and properly used by business people. These criteria may sound simple, but they are the fundamental obstacles companies face in building the information assets of the twenty-first century. On-line information is increasingly available in a number of markets. Networks and communications systems are being built to allow greater capability of information transfer. Many nations are changing their fundamental communications architecture to fibre optics to enable their businesses to have access to the best competitive and market information.

On-line information systems

Various organizations have large databases of information stored on computers. For a fee, the user can gain access to this information via a personal computer and a telephone line. The user can then display the information on his PC, print it out or download the information on to a disk for future reference. The fee usually covers the amount of time the user is connected to the database plus the amount of information extracted. It is cost-effective if the user is trained in the skill of searching for information, but less so if one spends a great deal of time working round the system to try and find what it is that is really wanted. Many businesses prefer to pay for the services of an information broker, or a skilled organization that will do the searching in databases on the client's behalf. Most business and management institutes offer such services and business libraries can provide information about brokers and the on-line information systems that are on offer. These can range from news services to company financial information to market research. The choice is expanding all the time.

However, there is another obstacle to managers' abilities to develop information assets. The value perceived by business people of information changes depend on their management focus and not enough managers are sensitive to the value of information. Relatively few people are information literate and even fewer understand the relevance of information to their business visions.

The business vision provides a fabric of cultural objectives (such as 'how we treat our customers') into which management can weave strategic business information objectives. Part of the effort is to understand the impact of systems on the direction and future of the business. Executives can imagine 'what if' scenarios such as 'What if we had a sound communications infrastructure from the field to head office that would deliver real-time customer purchase information; how would that change the way our business operates?' Examining the impact of systems helps executives and managers understand the 'technology context' of the business vision so that the various systems can be woven into the fabric of the company.

Ultimately, linking IT to the strategic programme is a way of building the company's global information assets. As we move into the information age of the twenty-first century, this could be the most important investment a firm makes.

Management View 5

Professor Tawfik Jelassi, Technology Management Area, INSEAD, Fontainebleau, France

(Professor Jelassi's current research work investigates the strategic uses of information technology and the development of decision and negotiation support systems, Daniels, 1992.)

Back in the 1960s the strategic dimension of IT was largely made up of operational systems of which production processing systems constituted a large part. By the mid-1980s and 1990s, the competitive landscape and rules of industry were and are being changed by the strategic role of IT. The airlines started new ways of leveraging information when they realized what a goldmine of information they were sitting on with their seat reservations systems. This is the strategic realization that many managers fail to make: information available within the company has value. The extra step taken by management to massage this information and to make it meaningful to the business context is the major strategic challenge. By making use of shared databases and distributed processing, American Airlines changed the rules of the marketplace *vis-à-vis* the competition. American accommodated all types of customers better by creating the frequent flier programme and by the leveraged use of their yield management system.

Otis Elevator France in 1992 provides an interesting case in Europe because of what Otis Elevator France has done to enhance a worldwide transaction processing system for local advantage. They began working with OTISLINE which is a shared database that holds an historic record of each elevator sold and the maintenance performed on that machine. Whenever a customer calls Otis Elevator, the profile of the unit – where it is located, how old it is, when it was last repaired, the mechanic in charge – is available to allow Otis immediately to despatch a mechanic for maintenance. Customer responsiveness was made a critical strategic weapon.

The enhancement that Otis Elevator France made further improved responsiveness. They implemented remote elevator maintenance (REM), this is a new service which provides pre-emptive maintenance. Before an elevator breaks down, a mechanic is despatched to repair the part that is about to

continues

continued

break down. This occurs 24 hours a day throughout the year. In many cases the customer does not even have to be told that a repair was made. What makes this possible is that Otis Elevator France has installed a chip in each elevator with sensors that monitor status information and relays that information back to Otis's central computer. Effectively, each elevator has a diagnostic unit providing information on-line. So when a part is slowing down or about to break, Otis France is warned ahead of time. This is a simple concept, but one that has had a big impact on the market because of the improvement in quality beyond the capabilities of the competition.

Otis Elevator France is also working on how to tie together different functions of the company, for example, providing the equipment salesforce with the necessary computing power to access information about current pricing systems and other services and to enable the sales person to respond to customer requests in the sales meeting. With the availability of this information, the timeframe between the customer request and the product and service offer is reduced. The salesperson can make an immediate offer without having to go through headquarters. This reduces the sales lead time significantly, from over a month to just a few hours. Once the sale has taken place, the information is then forwarded to central databases to which all other functions have access. Sales people can see the status of orders and when the production service contract was entered so that management can follow up and through. All these subsequent benefits are gained.

In future there will be further challenges and obstacles. We are moving towards the knowledge-based enterprise. We are no longer in the time when the database enterprise or information-based enterprise had an advantage. The issue is how to gain value and expertise from people from all over the company using information. The knowledge-based company has managers who know how to leverage knowledge for people who need it. There are three challenges here: (1) deciding how to acquire that knowledge with the help of the technology, (2) deciding how that knowledge can be understood and sufficiently used to provide the work with opportunities to add value, and (3) deciding not only how to align business strategy with the information technology plan, but also how to align the organizational structure to take the largest benefits of the new ways of doing business for the organization as a whole. Those companies that are able to get the leading benefits of technology are those that have aligned these three elements. Those that fail are those that did not pay attention to the organization restructuring or neglected education and training and met with resistance.

I call this operating 3-D and in parallel. Potential benefits and potential gains are at each of the individual, organizational and business levels. The pitfalls and dangers for top management are: (1) to be aware of the potential, (2) to be committed, and (3) to be involved. Because of the strategic dimension, these are the challenges to top management.

Bruno Grob, the CEO of Otis Elevator France has been promoted to CEO of Otis Elevator Europe. The company is trying to copy the French

continues

continued

experience with the new systems to become a European experience. Mr Grob describes the benefits he sees:

The competitive advantage doesn't come from the tool (the computer system). The tool is a tool, and the tool will remain a tool ... The tool should be served by a strategy, by a human resource, training, motivation and anything else ... The tool itself won't create the strategy, the motivation, the teamwork. The tool itself will create nothing. If it comes within a strategy, then it's outstanding; but it has to be prepared far in advance (Loebbecke, 1992).

At Otis, the links between the business, organization and technology have been well thought out, well established. There is a clear strategy with motivated individuals especially at the top.

We see a handful of companies using on-line transaction processing (OLTP) strategically. Others are hesitating about how to begin or manage it, but the competitive situation is that the companies are driving down a one-way street. If they begin to invest and do not see immediate advantages, they should not necessarily back up, but continue to get the benefits. In other words, the strategic trend of information technology will continue. Companies that do not accept the challenge will be at a disadvantage. It's a question of survival.

Companies often have five competitive objectives that illustrate the importance of information management: improving customer service, improving the time taken to bring a new product or service to market, improving quality, improving management communication and increasing global reach. Below are a few examples of companies who are using information to competitive advantage.

Improving customer service

In communication, the Dutch Post, Telephone and Telegraph company (PTT) has just launched two new products to gain competitive advantage. 'Teleguide' is a videotext system with which customers can peruse telephone number directories. Itemized billing offers business customers a chance to track the records of their telephone calls. Although these two products have been offered in other markets, these are two new information product offerings in Holland. The Dutch PTT developed these capabilities in an effort to prepare for the deregulation of the Dutch communications industries which will allow companies from other countries to compete. Competitive value is relative to the competitive environment.

Many banks advertise a 24-hour customer service hot-line to answer any query the customer may have. Being able to call the bank to ask questions about their account at any time of day is particularly attractive to people who work during the day and cannot always find time within the work day to conduct their banking business. While automated teller machines (ATMs) provide access to cash, the 24-hour customer service hot-lines provide extra help with electronic transfers of funds and account balance checks. If the customer has questions that a member of staff must answer, the customer can choose to exit from the electronic query process and signal for intervention from a bank employee. This is an example of a company extending its service capability by embedding IT in the product and service bundle.

Improving time-to-market

Companies are trying to decrease the time it takes to bring products to market. To accomplish this, automobile companies in Japan form teams of designers and manufacturers to design and produce new models. They form close-knit units that share information on an ongoing basis. They use state of the art computer systems to design the car in three dimensions, to test prototype designs and to determine the best mode for production and delivery. Many industries are attempting to find ways to overlap design and manufacturing tasks to bring products and services to market more quickly.

Improving quality

Improving the quality of products and services is dependent upon the knowledge that is held within the firm about how to create and make products and services. Improving the techniques for holding knowledge and increasing the learning of the organization is a valuable asset-generating activity of the firm. Transferring knowledge and know-how among human beings across the organization via the use of shared databases enhances the ability of the firm to uphold and raise high quality standards.

Improving management communication

Managers who share information can help each other to make decisions. The more managers in the create-to-make process lend a perspective on problem-solving at any particular point, the better the firm is at problem-solving. Systems are being built to support simultaneous communications and decision-making across the business processes.

Increasing global reach

As global competition increases, executives and managers are looking to expand their ability to communicate on a worldwide basis. Finding the best ideas in the world is an information management quest. Translating these ideas into marketable products released into markets where demand is high at the right time requires a good understanding of market conditions. Environmental scanning of markets and resources provides management teams with a rich reservoir of material with which to build competitive advantage.

Action checklist

(1)   Does your company attempt to bundle information into product and service offerings?

(2)   What are the key points of event in your business?

(3)   Are there information barriers among the key cycles in your business?

(4)   How is customer information used in your business?

(5)   What competitive advantage does (or could) your company build with information?

References

Daniels, N. Caroline. (1992). *On-Line Transaction Processing: Enhancing Your Business Strategy.* London: Economist Intelligence Unit Special Report No. P666

Loebbecke, C. (1992). Staying at the top with Otis Elevator – sustaining a competitive advantage through IT. Winner of the 1992 European Foundation for Management Development Technology Award

5

Managing the development of an IT strategy

- Involving all key decision-making staff is essential in the early stages of determining strategy. The cross-functional nature of IT requires wide ownership of the business vision.

- Strategic vision must include indications of how it is to be implemented.

- Implementation depends on focusing activity, setting quantifiable targets and timeframes.

- IT applications must be prioritized in line with strategic objectives.

- IT programmes must be clearly communicated throughout an organization so that each manager and employee is clear about their role in the process.

- The main causes of failure in IT investment are (a) not understanding how IT can impact on an industry or business; (b) not balancing an organization's IT requirements with its skill base; (c) trying to manage all IT projects in the same way.

- The stages of IT investment in the company can be charted and monitored and used as a benchmark for a company's IT progress against competitors.

- IT systems age, and their competitive value changes over time. IT is always a continuous, long-term investment of people and money.

People matter most

Translating business information needs into a sustainable IT strategy depends on key people within the organization. Creating the right team is of paramount importance. Time spent on this issue early in the process is paid back a thousand-fold when it is time to sell the vision to the rest of the organization. In essence, unless all a company's major stakeholders are involved in the visioning sessions, carrying the vision through will become a back-breaking process.

Getting started

Many companies will have vision, mission, or business purpose statements already in existence, and it is important to include these as a basis for the visioning sessions. Strategic and tactical plans already in operation that state the company's strategic intent should be used as a platform. Most often the visioning team will consist of top level executive staff and department heads. These executives will communicate with key members of their management teams throughout the process.

Members of the executive staff must make it clear that the visioning team's mandate is not only to develop the vision, but also to determine how to disseminate it into the value system and culture of the company. As a result, participants will think more about involving other constituents throughout the visioning process to ensure that they have had a part in forming the shape of the vision.

Communicating the activities of the visioning team is important, even early on. The more that management knows about the visioning process, the more time they have to assimilate the major messages and to accommodate change in their activities. One company called this communication and involvement activity 'walking the halls' which meant engaging the informal communications systems to spread the word about the changes that were occurring. These informal communication systems exist in every company and it is important to include them in the process, allowing the visioning teams to spend time consciously deciding what to communicate through the 'jungle drums' of the organization.

Developing a new business vision

Developing a vision is a starting point to integrating strategic planning efforts. Brain-storming sessions to discuss the major directions of the company should take place, involving senior management usually at board level. An example would be the New York Life business vision, shown below. The NYL mission statement states how the company will compete and create competitive advantage, improve productivity and achieve management effectiveness, as well as noting a commitment to technology.

Mission statement of New York Life Insurance Company

The following mission statement sets forth the principles under which New York Life operates and defines the company's goals. New York Life will:

- produce and sell a wide and comprehensive range of competitive, high-quality financial products and services and information in the USA and Canada
- use its field representatives as major systems of distribution
- maintain and enhance its financial soundness and integrity; recognize the trust placed in it, the duty to deal fairly, the responsibility to provide good service; preserve its ability to meet all of its obligations to policy owners at the lowest possible cost
- seek maximum, real, orderly growth in its current operations through profitable, prudent expansion and diversification
- lead in the use of modern technology to run its business
- provide a corporate culture that will encourage an efficient, creative workplace, and provide increasing opportunities for a motivated, enthusiastic workforce, including fair treatment in hiring and promotion practices
- recognize its responsibility to maintain the highest level of good citizenship within the communities in which it operates.

Visions create a clear framework for the business. The vision process must articulate strategic intent in such a way that managers who are implementing the vision have a clear understanding of tangible objectives. The business vision provides a fabric of cultural objectives against which management can weave business objectives. By developing a new business vision, the importance of information to the business and the role of business IT becomes clear. For New York Life it means providing excellent information concerning customers to agents in the field.

Part of the effort is to understand the impact of systems on the direction and future of the business. Executives can imagine 'what if' scenarios, such as 'If we had a sound communications infrastructure from the field to head office, what would that do to the business?'. Examining the impact of systems helps executives and managers understand the technology context of the business vision so that the various systems can be woven into the fabric of the company.

Other characteristics and concerns extracted from vision process workshops range over a wide area and have IT implications:

- How will we differentiate ourselves in the marketplace? Will we communicate with our customers better or fulfil orders more quickly than our competitors?
- We need to achieve x per cent market share by concentrating on customer relationships with certain segments. How will we achieve this? How do we identify the patterns, characteristics and desires of our customers as accurately as possible? Can we anticipate the market?
- Our products will have a long life and will be serviced for the life of the product at a minimal rate. What does this mean for customer service? How can we keep track of the products that we have sold – our installed base?
- We will maintain high productivity by investing in projects that will bring us high returns. What management information do we need to be able to monitor a project's progress?
- The profit per employee should be six per cent. How can we leverage the human resources of the firm to achieve this?
- Time-to-market advantage will be achieved by getting our products to market within six months of conception. How will we set up the network of processes that must take place as efficiently and effectively as possible?
- Our costs will be medium-range, probably not the lowest, but we will make an effort to keep costs as low as possible while achieving the level of service our customers expect. Do we have opportunities to change the cost structure of our business?
- Organization effectiveness will be improved by the excellent coordination of work processes. A good atmosphere and cooperation from the workers are essential. Employees must generate a 'want to solve' attitude. To this end, our employees must be kept 'in the loop' of vital communications. How do we ensure that communications of our major decisions are made?

Discussing the relative importance of information in each of these areas helps to bring out the dependence of the business on business IT and focus management's attention on what needs to be done. Figure 5.1 gives an overview of the whole visioning process. As management discusses the

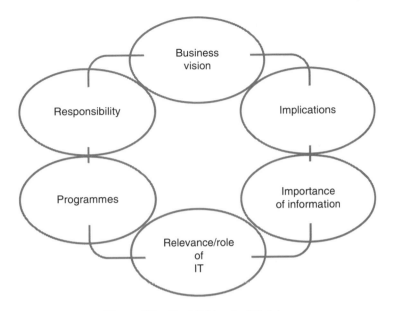

Figure 5.1   Establishing the IT vision.

relative importance of aspects of the vision, they are making value judgements about the priorities of investment in business information. Many executive teams then go through a prioritizing session stating the key elements of the vision and describing exactly what needs to be done for the vision to be achieved. Stating the importance and role of information in achieving each aspect of the vision places IT firmly in the business vision context. Chartham Paper Mills went through this process, described in Case 5.1.

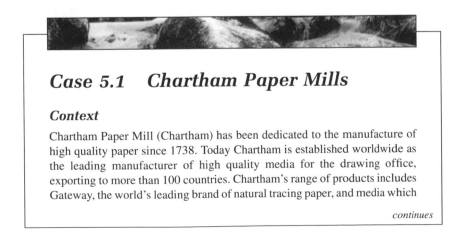

Case 5.1   Chartham Paper Mills

Context

Chartham Paper Mill (Chartham) has been dedicated to the manufacture of high quality paper since 1738. Today Chartham is established worldwide as the leading manufacturer of high quality media for the drawing office, exporting to more than 100 countries. Chartham's range of products includes Gateway, the world's leading brand of natural tracing paper, and media which

continues

continued

are setting the standards for the rapidly changing imaging technology of the 1990s. Chartham Paper Mill has recently become part of the major US group, James River Corporation.

Why change?

When James River bought Chartham, it was reliant on its former parent company, Wiggins Teape, for use of its centralized IT facilities. Most management information and financial systems would disappear as of 1 January 1988. The remainder of the managerial systems ran on local personal computers.

Vision

Management went through a visioning process to identify the business and IT strategy. The business vision at Chartham was to be the world's leading provider of high quality media for the drawing office. Chartham prides itself on maintaining excellent relationships with customers, often creating new products and improvements in conjunction with them. With this comes a commitment to the use of information systems. As Harry Constable, managing director of Chartham, said:

> We are making use of the latest advances and systems to continue our long tradition of quality and care into the future. Every aspect of our activity is part of a total Quality Management programme, a culture focused on meeting our clients' specific requirements first time, on time, every time. We have invested in introducing computer technology throughout the mill. This includes the latest computer-controlled manufacturing and quality control techniques to maintain the highest possible standards for our complete range of products.

What Chartham did

PCs at Chartham had been put to innovative uses, particularly in the quality control area. Chartham's management wanted to build on the innovative characteristics of the existing systems to provide a mill-wide system that would provide business information for every aspect of the business in such a way that information is up-to-date; is instantly available (to those with the authority to know) at the workplace; and can be input or output from or to other people's systems.

The IT strategy identified areas of the business to focus on. The company should:

- concentrate on systems that support the business needs
- minimize duplication of data through centralized databases
- commence with replacement system modules necessitated by the takeover
- proceed to areas of cost saving
- use systems packages with absolutely minimal essential changes
- use packages which could be integrated

continues

continued

- use common, proven hardware which could be integrated
- build on to existing personal computer and local networking skills
- use corporate (James River) solutions and resources, if possible.

Mike Fitzpatrick, systems manager, said:

> Mill-wide systems is wider than you think. It includes quality data, accounting, marketing, sales, payroll, operations, currency management, human resources and machine scheduling. Everything that stirs in the place is part of the total system. Above all we wanted integration in our systems to support the vision, the common thread that runs through every business process here.

Chartham appointed Mike Fitzpatrick as the systems manager and hired IT professionals to work with independent consultants to implement the systems. The parent company, James River, had recruited an MIS director at business group level to initiate and centrally coordinate Chartham's activity with the parent. The decision was made to avoid tailormade systems and to use packages that could be tailored to integrate.

Andrew Rigby, financial director, discussed the package selection option: 'There is a wider range of customers using packages now than five years ago. Implementing a packaged system has certain advantages; there is support for the company using it; software support with the package; and a user community of support with other companies.'

Chartham's PCs were the platform using financial and production process packages linked via Ethernet to the DEC Vax. Since the company has an excellent relationship with its local Olivetti dealer, many of the PCs were Olivetti. The key to success, according to Mike Fitzpatrick, 'is that we set standards for the tools we chose and that the business community here is highly computer literate. Everyone uses PCs. No one is frightened of IT.'

Outcome

Mike Fitzpatrick said:

> Information is now available faster in a more consistent, reliable and easily accessible way than before. Chartham is moving away from paper-based processes to being able to access everything on real-time databases through a network of PCs. This has made a world of difference to our business. There have been enormous gains in personal productivity. In the accounts area, we have had a 25 per cent decrease in staff; other gains have been made in the commercial sales order processing area. We have reduced office and shop floor staff while generating greater revenue and profit than ever before. We have eliminated some externally purchased services, such as in the area of the preparation of export documents. The choice of shipping carrier and other details are readily available to distribution. We create all of our own presentation graphics.

continues

continued

All senior directors are PC users. We even do all of our own corporate brochures. We use printed barcoding labels that are attached to our products and that we make to order. Of course we are constantly enhancing our CAD systems for engineering and maintenance: engineering systems – that is the heart of our business.

Future

Mike Fitzpatrick said:

The future will be continual change and growth. Our motto is to 'find a better way'. We are ahead of our competitors in the use of information systems. We're world leaders in the products we produce and in the technology we use to get products to our customers. Chartham's culture is committed to that business purpose.

Linking IT to the strategic programme

To evaluate the importance of IT to each business objective, management must think about what the company should do to achieve that objective and grade the importance of information accordingly. For example, if management decides that to differentiate the company in the marketplace it must be the lowest cost producer, the question becomes, 'What must be done to achieve that?'

A financial services company's management decided that enabling its customer service representatives to process their own requests for product would make an enormous saving in back office (administrative) costs, as well as going some way towards another business objective, that of achieving immediate response to customer requests. Another way to lower costs would be to transfer all paper files to electronic images, which would be made available through networks of graphic databases. The company was based in a major city and the space saving alone for the filing of papers was enormous. A third way would be to allow managers to access management information systems that showed work in progress, thereby freeing customer account representatives from an onslaught of *ad hoc* sales reporting requests that had caused expensive and tedious interruptions and bottlenecks to sales operations. All three activities (Figure 5.2) had implications for how IT would be used in the firm.

Ranking the business projects and considering what the company would actually have to do to achieve its objectives allows management to prioritize the full programme of efforts and objectives. In exploring what has to be done in terms of IT, making use of the information attributes mentioned in Chapter 3 (currency, content, quality, flexibility, importance relating to the process and scalability) helps to refine the assessment of the effort required to carry out the objectives. For example, in the case above the customer representatives would

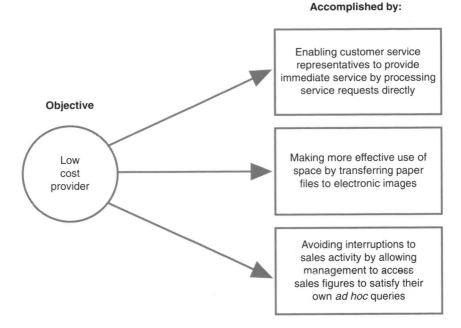

Accomplished by:

Enabling customer service representatives to provide immediate service by processing service requests directly

Objective

Low cost provider

Making more effective use of space by transferring paper files to electronic images

Avoiding interruptions to sales activity by allowing management to access sales figures to satisfy their own *ad hoc* queries

Figure 5.2   Accomplishing business objectives with IT.

need current information about products and customers to be able to serve the customer directly. Except for the task of transferring the paper files to electronic images, the IT involved may not have to supply immediate and current information for all files.

Having defined what must be achieved and what the company must do to accomplish these goals, the next step is to define where in the organization these objectives can be met.

Translating the vision into actionable programmes

Translating the vision into action involves articulating who will be involved, what their roles will be and setting out measures that can be used as milestones or guides to gauge progress. David Norton, president of Nolan, Norton & Co., invented a methodology he called 'developing the "strategic vectors" of a firm' (see Figure 5.3) (Norton, 1987). 'To be of value, a vision must be translated: it must focus the organization, set quantifiable targets and establish time horizons.' Executives often have visions of the business that they believe are clearly articulated but which are, to the managers who must meet the objectives, obscure. Many companies can get into a situation where the vision is 'in the minds' of top management, but perhaps less clear to the rest of the people in the company. Dave Norton described the problem:

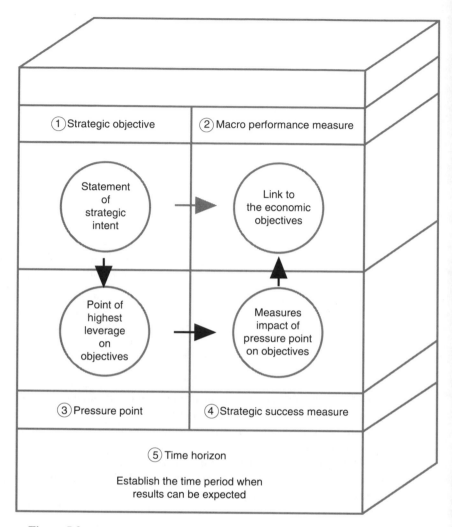

Figure 5.3   A strategic vector. (*Source:* David P. Norton (1988). *Stage by Stage.* Nolan, Norton & Co.: Lexington, Massachusetts.)

At a company that I will call Powco, a large utility company, the vision statement clearly identified the company's intention to 'lead the industry' in two critical dimensions: customer satisfaction and financial return to investors. The intention 'to lead the industry' set out a stretch target that pushed the organisation. The vision statement was then translated into a set of strategic objectives, one of which was to improve customer relations (see Figure 5.4). But although this objective was entirely consistent with the strategic vision, it was not sufficient to guide more specific actions.

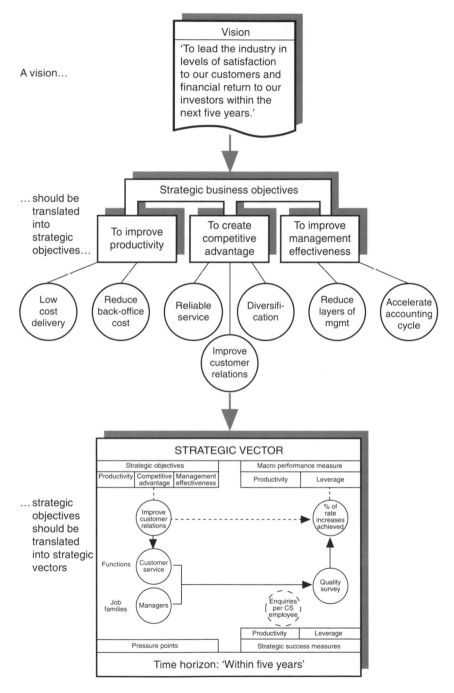

A vision...

> **Vision**
>
> 'To lead the industry in levels of satisfaction to our customers and financial return to our investors within the next five years.'

... should be translated into strategic objectives...

Strategic business objectives

To improve productivity

To create competitive advantage

To improve management effectiveness

Low cost delivery

Reduce back-office cost

Reliable service

Diversifi- cation

Reduce layers of mgmt

Accelerate accounting cycle

Improve customer relations

... strategic objectives should be translated into strategic vectors

STRATEGIC VECTOR

Strategic objectives			Macro performance measure	
Productivity	Competitive advantage	Management effectiveness	Productivity	Leverage

Improve customer relations

% of rate increases achieved

Functions — Customer service

Quality survey

Job families — Managers

Enquiries per CS employee

	Productivity	Leverage
Pressure points	Strategic success measures	

Time horizon: 'Within five years'

Figure 5.4 The translation of Powco's vision. (*Source:* David P. Norton (1988). *Stage by Stage*. Nolan, Norton & Co.: Lexington, Massachusetts.)

The strategic objectives

The vision needed to be more fully and explicitly described so that management could take action. The vision needed a statement of the strategic objectives.

The macro performance measure

This establishes a link between the strategic objective and the economic goals of the company. At Powco there was a direct link between customer satisfaction and the pricing structure. Since rates were set by a regulatory body, and since a scientific survey of customer satisfaction was used as a major input to this decision, it was reasonable to expect that higher levels of customer satisfaction would result in higher rate increases. The macro performance measure for Powco was: percentage of requested rate increases achieved.

The pressure point

This is the organizational area that has the greatest impact on the ability to accomplish the objective. If a company has limited resources, where should management apply them to accomplish the objective? It might be a critical function, job family (job classification) or process. For Powco the pressure points were the customer service function and the manager job family.

The strategic success measure

This is the impact of the pressure point on the strategic objective. It provides a means of quantifying the results of actions and investments being made to influence the pressure point. At Powco the investments being made in the customer service department were intended to improve customer satisfaction, as measured by the results of the customer quality survey. This also directly links the macro performance measure: if the quality survey improves, there should be an increase in the percentage of rate increases achieved.

The time horizon

This links a time dimension to the effort. It is of little value to set clear targets if the timing is ambiguous. When John Kennedy committed the USA to 'put a man on the moon by the end of the decade', he not only established a clear, focused objective, but also added a sense of urgency.

Translating the objective into IT programmes provides a cluster for strategic investment. In Powco's case, management translated the business objective into clearly articulated plans for IT, training and external variables that they could not control (see Figure 5.5). The plans for IT were for a range of systems including a customer billing system and a system to allow customers to pay directly by telephone.

Having driven the vision into actionable programmes, management can then assign responsibility.

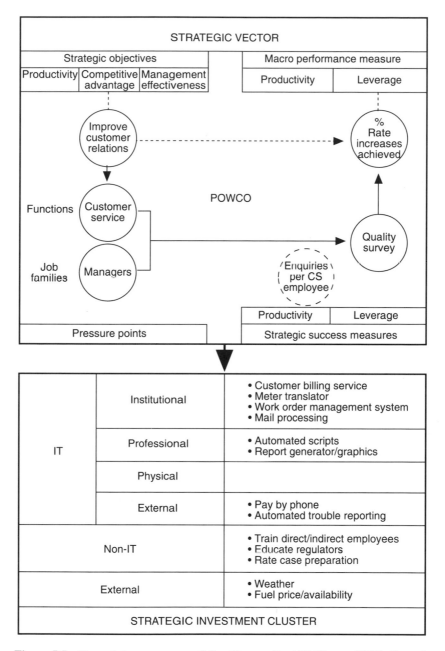

Figure 5.5   Powco's investment portfolio. (*Source:* David P. Norton (1988). *Stage by Stage*. Nolan, Norton & Co.: Lexington, Massachusetts.)

Assigning responsibility and sustaining consistent progress

Every manager must understand their mandate for carrying out business programmes. As these programmes are driven forward, incorporating IT projects, a learning process for management develops that integrates IT with the business objectives on a day-to-day basis.

Developing a call for action that addresses a change in the way the company does business requires a great deal of communication and involvement at all levels of the organization. This communication can take many forms: one-to-one meetings, company-wide manager conferences or videotapes, to name a few. The most effective methods integrating business and IT activities are those that require active participation. As organizations take advantage of the new capabilities available with IT, making IT an integral part of management will increase in importance.

Getting it wrong

In 1981 Professor Warren McFarlan published an article in the *Harvard Business Review* citing examples of companies' failure to manage their investment in IT effectively. The single examples he cited then reflect whole classes of companies now. For example, even with the development of open systems, companies still experience great pain in trying to switch from one hardware vendor to the next. The process of switching is inevitably more difficult, more expensive and more time consuming than companies foresee; somewhat more complicated than untangling a ball of string.

Other companies face problems such as beginning development projects with an expectation that the investment involved would be in a specified range, only to find that the amount required to 'finish' the project is far greater. A major UK bank is in the process of restructuring its back office processes to make use of IT. Much of the processing will be done by computer signals instigated from the front office, the customer sales and service area. The chief information officer mentioned in a quiet voice that it would be a miracle if the project did not take the majority of the bank's financial resources during the next few years.

Yet other companies find that the backlog of requested systems mounts as aging systems deliver less than expected. As well as delivering diminished benefits to the company, the projects are monopolizing IT resources. Business management has always had trouble in forecasting and anticipating the impact of systems on the business and how systems develop throughout the company over a given period of time.

These problems – anticipating complexity, planning appropriate investment and applying resources effectively – recur often enough to raise the question: 'Why do businesses seem to face the same problems over and again and yet still fall down in the implementation of the fundamentals of managing IT?' McFarlan (1981) posed this question 12 years ago: 'Given more than 20 years of IS experience, the question is "Why?" '. There is as yet no answer.

There are three main reasons for the lack of success in managing business IT. The first is that managers fail to assess how their business and IT interact in order to gain an accurate picture of where the business is building from and to measure the distance required to get to where they want to be. Second, few companies carry out an assessment of the powers of supply and demand of IT in their business. Exploring this balance can give an accurate appraisal of the current state of IT: the portfolio of skills and computer power to be matched against the needs of the user community. Finally, there is a lack of understanding that different projects require different investment and management approaches. A fatal flaw in managing business IT is to manage each project in the same way.

Managers can learn to manage the IT effort as a portfolio of business technology. Building a business model can help to give an idea of what that portfolio looks like.

Stages in the use of IT

One fundamental difficulty in managing IT is that management do not have a framework for measuring and tracking progress. Richard Nolan of the Harvard Business School has developed a descriptive theory based on his observations that companies pass through stages of experience in learning how to manage IT. The 'stages theory' is illustrated in Figure 5.6. By identifying the stage(s) a company is in, management can develop plans based on an overall corporate profile of business IT management.

The stages theory

The six stages illustrated here can be further divided into two areas: the data processing (DP) era stages and the IT era stages. The DP era (stages 1–3) refers to the time when data processing management focused on managing the data processing resource itself: DP staff, the computers and the software. In the IT era (stages 4–6), the focus is the effectiveness of the systems in integrating capability with business processes and the overall business objectives.

Stage 1: initiation

Operational level business functions are automated to some degree. The first systems typically relate to the accounting function, that is payroll, inventory,

Figure 5.6 The six stages of data-processing growth. (*Source:* Richard Nolan. Managing the crisis in data processing. *Harvard Business Review*, 115–26, March–April 1987.)

Growth processes

	Stage 1 Initiation	Stage 2 Contagion	Stage 3 Control	Stage 4 Integration	Stage 5 Data administration	Stage 6 Maturity
Applications portfolio	Functional cost reduction applications	Proliferation	Upgrade documentation and restructure existing applications	Retrofitting existing applications using database technology	Organization Integration of applications	Application integration 'mirroring' information flows
DP organization	Specialization for technological learning	User-oriented programmers	Middle management	Establish computer utility and user account teams	Data administration	Data resource management
DP planning and control	Lax	More lax	Formalized planning and control ▲ Transition point	Tailored planning and control systems	Shared data and common systems	Data resource strategic planning
User awareness	"Hands off"	Superficially enthusiastic	Arbitrarily held accountable	Accountability learning	Effectively accountable	Acceptance of joint user and data processing accountability
Level of DP expenditures						

accounts payable and receivable. Business managers are relatively uninvolved in the information design process, while DP professionals spend most of their time with programming code and machines.

Stage 2: contagion

Management demands automated information to improve the currency of many other functional areas. Business managers begin to appreciate the speed of data processing. The DP staff are building skills, beginning to experiment with programs which serve other purposes than the strict transaction-efficiency operations. Control of both user demand and the experience of DP staff eventually gets out of hand and management reacts with control measures to bring the demand and supply of automation in line.

Stage 3: control

This stage combines the development of measurement techniques for data processing resources, such as how many programs are written, with a growth of awareness in business managers that managing data resources is important to the effectiveness of the business as a whole. Usually a profusion of data-management and database issues are discussed. As the complexity of the information management requests rises, the data processing staff try to assimilate base technologies. Applications of data processing begin to span operational functions, such as order processing, managing data from customer sales, inventory and delivery.

The company has entered the IT era. For many companies this began in the late 1970s and is still going on. Access to information, rather than playing a purely supportive role to the business, is vital in many areas. Information becomes a strategic consideration, an element of strategic advantage or competitive parity. Management begin to look at IT as an investment rather than a cost, and justify expenditure on a capability basis, that is what the systems will enable the business to do. Management attitudes to IT shift. Business managers become more involved with the management of information related to their concerns. Many more managers discover they have a stake in how information is managed and the priorities placed on developing systems.

Stage 4: integration

Business managers begin to take leadership into consideration when combining IT and business resources. Managers begin to design systems of information with IT staff.

Stage 5: data administration

A greater investigation into the value of information to the business is generated, and a greater focus on achieving demonstrable benefits to the company obsesses management.

Stage 6: maturity

The application of information systems mirrors the business processes. In many cases, the business processes have been reorganized taking into account the capabilities of IT.

The stages theory is a fundamental concept in understanding the management of IT in business. The theory marked the beginning of the management of IT as a business asset because the framework enables managers to measure IT resources and the effectiveness of delivering valuable information to the business. This concept is referred to throughout the rest of the book.

Richard Nolan (1979), commenting on the competitive progression of IT and the stages theory, said: 'If you ask me how many stages there are, I would have to say that there are an infinite number. The business environment of IT is constantly changing. There is always one more step.' To understand how IT develops its many lives, managers must discover how long they can rely on any particular phase of a system's life.

Benchmarking how a company fares

Stage status is an important consideration in business strategy. Using Nolan's theory, an interesting measure of progress in managing business IT can be made by comparing a company's IT with that of other businesses (see Figure 5.7). For example, if IT expenditure is tracking the rate of growth of sales, the company is most probably either initiating (stage 1) an IT effort, or has assimilated the technologies and is taking advantage of IT in maturity (stage 6).

It is likely that different parts of a company are in different stages of IT development, but different functions will converge as the company integrates its technology. To evaluate how a company is faring against the competition, managers should ask what activities the competitor can carry out.

- Stage 1. Does the competitor have an accurate picture of its accounts receivable and payable? Does it manage its inventory levels well? How does it manage its working capital?
- Stage 2. Does the competitor process orders efficiently? Does it make mistakes which get through to customers? Are any operational level activities in warehousing or manufacturing automated?
- Stage 3. Does the competitor have a database of customer information? How quickly can it answer routine questions about its operations?
- Stage 4. Does the competitor recognize customer service and other market-driven indicators as important to its business? Can it respond to demand flexibly?

Figure 5.7 Benchmarks of the six stages. (*Source:* Richard Nolan. Managing the crisis in data processing. *Harvard Business Review*, 115–26, March–April 1987.)

	Stage 1 Initiation	Stage 2 Contagion	Stage 3 Control	Stage 4 Integration	Stage 5 Data administration	Stage 6 Maturity
First-level analysis						
DP expenditure benchmarks	Tracks rate of sales growth	Exceeds rate of sales growth	Is less than rate of sales growth	Exceeds rate of sales growth	Is less than rate of sales growth	Tracks rate of sales growth
Technology benchmarks	100% batch processing	80% batch processing, 20% remote job entry processing	70% batch processing, 15% database processing, 10% inquiry processing, 5% time-sharing processing	50% batch and remote job entry processing, 40% database and data communications processing, 5% personal computing, 5% minicomputer and micro-computer processing	20% batch and remote job entry processing, 60% database and data communications processing, 5% personal computing, 15% minicomputer and microcomputer processing	10% batch and remote job entry processing, 60% database and data communications processing, 5% personal computing, 25% minicomputer and microcomputer processing
Second-level analysis						
Applications portfolio		There is a concentration on labour-intensive automation, scientific support and clerical replacement	Applications move out to user locations for data generation and data use		Balance is established between centralized shared data/common system applications and decentralized user-controlled applications	
DP organization		Data processing is centralized and operates as a 'closed shop'	Data processing becomes data custodian. Computer utility established and achieves reliability	▲ **Transition point**	There is organizational implementation of the data resource management concept. There are layers of responsibility for data processing at appropriate organizational levels	
DP planning and control		Internal planning and control is installed to manage the computer. Included are standards for programming, responsibility accounting and project management		External planning and control are installed to manage data resources. Included are value-added user chargeback, steering committee and data administration		
User awareness		Reactive. End user is superficially involved. The computer provides more, better and faster information than manual techniques	Driving force. End user is directly involved with data entry and data use. End user is accountable for data quality and for value-added end use		Participation. End user and data processing are jointly accountable for data quality and for effective design of value-added applications	
Level of DP expenditures	Stage 1 Initiation	Stage 2 Contagion	Stage 3 Control	Stage 4 Integration	Stage 5 Data administration	Stage 6 Maturity

- Stage 5. Does the competitor segment the market effectively? Can it tailor products and services for customers?
- Stage 6. Is the competitor using information as a part of its product offering? Is it achieving competitive advantage because of its capability to manage IT as an integral part of its business?

Every good business manager has an idea of who the company's competitors are and how they are operating. Positioning the company with respect to its competition gives a picture of how information is managed in a particular industry.

The life of a system

The age of the corporate IT portfolio is also an important part of business information strategy. The length of a system's life varies. Systems that deliver sophisticated financial products may only be vital for a few months as markets change and the financial product itself is replaced, whereas the infrastructure of a warehousing system may last between five and ten years. Each system will have a life span dependent on the use to which the system is put, and the applicability of the logic of the information to the business.

The initial cycle of a system passes through many phases similar to the product development phases of any new product or service: conception, design and development; implementation; production; and audit. Ideally these phases mirror the process lifecycle of the company's products and services: birth, growth, maturity and decline.

Successful IT is a long-term programme. At any given time the company's portfolio of systems (opportunities for applying IT to the company's range of activities) should be at various stages of the system lifecycle. Some systems will be in development, while others will be fully operational.

Systems in the development phase can represent an expenditure range of approximately 12–30% of the IT budget, depending on what stage of IT the company is in. Development systems are new systems or systems that replace old systems. Maintenance and enhancement (20–30% of the IT budget) is the effort that goes into making minor changes to systems to increase functionality: that is, to modify the information logic for changing market conditions or to enhance the system's ease of use. Change control must be managed well during this phase. Finally, production systems are the systems that tick over like a clock, the core of a company's IT capability, representing 45–65% of the budget.

These estimates are rough rules of thumb. Additional investment guidelines indicate that the growth rate of systems is only sustainable for a certain period of time: that is, the company must assimilate the capability of new systems and use the systems as production systems before launching into new areas. Although the capacity for technological assimilation varies from company to company, unless the environment is going through exceptional change, the growth rate should not exceed 20% for more than four years in a row. Constant explosion of IT growth or wildly varying growth rates from year to year can throw a company's IT investment off course.

Equally, a company's investment in the technology and the people to operate the technology should grow at a rate that supports the assimilation process. A major part of an IT budget is devoted to training people to work with the technology. The 'people' investment is increasing as a percentage of the whole investment, as costs of technology decrease and as the need for skills increases. As a rough guide, approximately 30–50% of the IT spend relates to the technology, and 50–70% to the organizational aspects of the investment. These two aspects of the investment must be well integrated to provide an optimal return.

Action checklist

(1)   What stage of IT development is your company in? What stage are your competitors in? Is there a way to take advantage in your industry with IT?

(2)   How do your current IT plans fit in with the overall portfolio of investment your company has made? Can the business get to the position desired by building on the current foundation of the business?

(3)   How many different vision/business purposes does your company currently hold?

(4)   What are the company's key objectives? How dependent are these on information? What impact could IT have: change the way the process is carried out; improve efficiency; or provide an information-based characteristic to the product/service to enhance the product offering?

(5)   What are the actions the company must take to meet strategic objectives? How information dependent are these?

(6)   What are the key areas managers will come from to coordinate the vision programme description effort?

(7)   How will the programme be communicated to the organization? How will the different parts of the organization be involved?

(8)   Are the vision, key business objectives and roles defined in a tangible enough way for people to carry out the next steps of the process?

References

McFarlan, F. W. (1981). Portfolio approach to information systems. *Harvard Business Review*, 142–50, September–October

Nolan, R. (1987). Managing the crises in data processing. *Harvard Business Review*, 115–26, March–April

Norton, D. P. (1987). Strategic vectors: translating vision into action. *Stage by Stage*, **7**(3) Nolan, Norton & Co. Massachusetts, May–June

6

Analysing IT investment

- If inadequate resources are committed to IT worthwhile projects will fail.
- Everyone should be involved in the evaluation of the financial benefits of an IT project.
- Portfolios of systems must be well integrated with the company's overall business vision.
- Business and IT managers must have a clear idea of their roles and responsibilities in relation to IT expenditure.
- Companies need to know how much they are spending on IT throughout the organization; more should be spent in high priority areas of the business.
- It is most important to consider both the implicit costs (time spent planning and implementing systems) and the explicit costs (hardware, software, etc) in analysing investments.
- All major shareholders should be involved in planning projects in order of priority.
- To ensure a positive return on investment it is essential to get the whole organization excited about the potential of IT.

Management approaches to investment

> My boss says repeatedly that IT is of strategic significance and that
> this project is particularly important to the survival of the company.
> But when it comes to committing resources to the effort, I'm
> constrained, in terms of time, people and money. What does he expect
> me to do?

More often than many executives would care to admit, projects are given
the go-ahead by management without adequate resources in the hope that they
will succeed on the basis of natural selection; in other words the good projects
will attract the resources and succeed, the weaker projects will fail. However,
this course of action, or non-action since it represents a failure of management
decision-making, leaves many worthwhile projects open to a risk that may
prove to be critical. Projects may fail prematurely because of management's
lack of ability to prioritize investments. IT investments need to be managed as
effectively as other business assets. All business investments are linked to
strategic priorities, available resources and risk.

In order to achieve an effective IT implementation plan the project directors, the business leaders and the technology leaders all need to be involved in
the evaluation of the financial benefits, the match to business objectives, the
appraisal of intangible benefits and the estimation of the technical importance
of the portfolio of projects the company invests in. However well managers
may plan, aspects of the investment in IT remain unpredictable. Professor John
Stopford of the London Business School makes an important point:

> There are times when a firm does not know until it gains experience
> how the investment will affect the strategy. For example, while
> implementing plans to introduce a system for computer-aided manu-
> facturing, a company may begin to understand the increased benefits
> that would be brought about if design and manufacturing were
> integrated. This is a significant change to the strategy but one that
> would not have been realized without management having the
> experience of implementing IT in manufacturing and seeing other
> strategic possibilities once they were involved in the process.

At Benetton (see Case 6.1) management saw increased opportunities
for using IT by building on the IT strengths they already had. By combining
existing systems, management found a powerful new way to organize the
information in the business to identify potential sales, giving marketing a
clearer target.

John Bennett of Coopers & Lybrand Deloitte pointed out another pitfall in
implementing IT projects: that of failing to remember that implementing
strategic IT is like aiming at a moving target.

Having a good strategy is not the whole answer. IT plans have to leave room for market changes. The head office of an international company set out on a project to obtain a single world view of invoicing and client relationships. The company operated in two major market segments: the first was high margin/low volume, the second low margin/high volume. Because the latter was more readily understood, and hence reduced the initial IT project risk, management chose to concentrate systems efforts there.

The market moved. Overnight it became a market in surplus. Plants were mothballed as margins became non-existent. Managers looked at the IT system to see what they could salvage, but the system was so specifically tailored to the condition of the market that little of the effort could be saved.

Years ago project planning models were based on stability and lack of change within the IT plans. Today the amount of change occurring is equivalent to turbulence; even the relative stability required to build transaction systems is missing. Managers need to plan to place development efforts in areas that may serve multiple strategies and support market changes.

Case 6.1   Benetton

Context

Benetton was founded 25 years ago as a small family clothing business in northern Italy. Through the excellent and innovative nature of its designs, Benetton has grown to be a clothing business of international importance, with a market presence in 75 countries and a total of 5900 retail outlets. Its core business remains the creation (design), manufacture, marketing, distribution and retailing of fashion clothing, competing in the high-quality, medium-price market. Fashion is a seasonal business with two new 'collections' marketed each year, one covering the spring and summer seasons and the other the autumn and winter.

Manufacture is 91% Italian. Only 20% of this is in-house, the remaining 80% is subcontracted under the direct control of the group. Marketing and commercial control over the retail outlets is exercised through carefully

continues

continued

selected agents, of whom there are 73 worldwide. These agents are mostly connected with the Benetton family, which still runs the now public company, although they are separate legal entities in their own right. The agents 'show' each new collection to the retailers, who place their orders through them. They are responsible for setting up the retail franchises and often have an equity stake in them.

Selling is through exclusively Benetton retail outlets which are tied by a strict commercial franchise arrangement. Goods are delivered direct to these outlets and invoicing/payment is made from/to the relevant factories with commission then being paid to the agents. Difficulties are resolved by the agents who are in constant touch with the retail outlets in their areas.

Vision

The group sees IT as key to its operations and is constantly seeking new ways to capitalize on the competitive power of properly used technology-based business systems. As the use of computing increased during the company's years of growth and expansion, it was perceived that there was a need to speed up and decentralize the activities related to the collection of orders from the agents in view of the high volumes, many countries, time zone differences and production information needs involved.

Using PCs installed in agents' offices and the store-and-collect application within a van network, order-entry was always available because the network decoupled the central order-processing application at head office from the data entry at the agent. Orders were collected efficiently and assessed twice a day by the central computer.

Why change?

It was immediately found that sufficient data were available for good forecasts of total orders to be made by the tenth day in the ordering cycle, enabling faster purchasing decisions on raw materials and better forward production planning.

As implementation proceeded, it became clear that the business had invested in a tool which has considerable potential far beyond the original, limited requirement; it was perceived as the basis of an electronic commercial network, allowing the different business entities to communicate directly with each other.

What Benetton did

As a result, a new project was started in June 1986 with a new network architecture, a newly developed agent information system running on DOS and XENIX workstations and a communications system for the interchange, any to any, of mail, reports and files. This new system was introduced during 1987.

continues

continued

Functionally it provides facilities for controlled order-entry, order confirmations, colour ordering instructions, message interchange, orders to local plants as well as Italian factories and transfer of orders between plants. The internal agents' applications are file management of the order portfolio, customers, stock items and price lists, as well as portfolio analysis capabilities. The system connects factories and agents in 21 countries – Australia, Austria, Belgium, Canada, Dubai, France, Germany, Greece, Hong Kong, Holland, Italy, the Republic of Ireland, Japan, South Korea, Norway, Portugal, Spain, Sweden, Switzerland, the USA and the UK.

Benetton is an ambitious company. It recognizes that the market is limited and that, in certain countries, saturation is already being reached. Its future growth plans include extending the product range to incorporate, for example, footwear and fashion accessories. In the short term, as long as the volume of sales is proportional to the number of retail outlets, in the nearly saturated markets the only way to increase revenue is to increase sales volume per shop.

The shop owner, like any entrepreneur, is concerned with the profit of his or her business and would accept ordering more only on the most popular selling items in that period, and only if delivery was guaranteed within a few days.

The reassortment process, the mechanism of reordering the best selling items, is hard to manage when the dimension of business is limited, and is almost impossible in an international market with manufacturing volumes of more than 50 m pieces per year. However, it can be achieved if the company can:

- focus on a limited number of items, the ones identified as the most popular
- start the production in advance, forecasting the volumes
- push the market to order, through the agents, what is in production in a semi-finished state or in stock
- assure a quick delivery on a basis of first in, first out.

This will improve the shop owners' business and at the same time increase their sales volume and profit, because these items will be sold at full price.

Outcome and future

The commercial infrastructure connecting the 73 agents worldwide with the factories was already available and the implementation of the reassortment system required only six months, mainly to improve the information interchange between the commercial department and the agents.

The commercial department updates the agents daily on the reassortment offering in terms of items, volumes and time availability. The agents then choose the items of most interest to them, ring the shop owners to collect orders and forward them to Benetton through the network. Benetton

continues

continued

computers collect the orders three times a day and notify the agents immediately if their orders are accepted or not.

The reassortment orders are processed during the night. The next morning the production department receives instructions on finishing and packaging the goods and the forwarding department is informed of their estimated time of arrival from production in order to programme the dispatch.

The goods are forwarded on average three days after the order is received. Delivery to the shop takes five to six days in Europe and eight to nine days in the USA. The whole cycle takes less than twelve days.

In revenue terms, the business has doubled in size from L714bn in 1984 to L1657bn in 1988, while net income has tripled in the same period from L43bn to L115bn. In 1990 the reassortment sales volume will represent about 6% of total sales, improving the business by more than 3m pieces and $7bn.

To deliver the highest value, portfolios of systems must be well integrated with the overall business purposes, the changing business environment and the corporate culture and processes of the company. The thrust of the IT effort should be communicated well enough to make the entire organization adopt the effort wholeheartedly, thus contributing to a stronger linkage of business information and technology.

This chapter addresses four fundamental issues in the management of the IT investment:

- Who controls IT spending?
- How much should be spent?
- Planning projects in order of priority.
- How to ensure a positive return on investment.

Who controls IT spending?

The answer to this question in many organizations is 'no one'. Too often the management of the IT budget is left to managers who have only a partial view of the investment required. Business managers may have a view on what is needed in their own area and IT managers may have a view on the technology, but both may lack an overall perception of the opportunities for applying IT throughout the business.

At the implementation level, IT programmes must be carried out in conjunction with and in the context of changes to the business processes and organizational changes. Managers must have enough knowledge of the whole process to understand the part the IT projects will play and their importance to the business purpose. Building the strategic initiatives and the business information architecture will give management this knowledge.

Business managers' roles

Managers must also have a clear idea of their responsibilities and the roles they will play. For the business manager these are:

- project owner
- project participant
- project supporter or champion.

Project owner

The person who takes responsibility for ensuring that everyone who needs to be involved is involved; the project is realistically assessed in performance measurement terms; the project reaches its objectives; and the benefits of the project are communicated to the organization as a whole. Ultimately the project owner takes responsibility for the project.

A good rule adopted by some companies is that every project lasting more than three to four days must have a project owner. If it does not, the project should not be undertaken.

Project participant

A person called in by the project owner to contribute his or her experience and perspective to the project. In particular, if a project spans functional boundaries, representatives from many departments will be involved to ensure that the project meets the goals of the function or process.

Project supporter

A business manager judged to be critical to the acceptance and running of the project. Project supporters represent many levels of the company. A senior executive serves as project champion if the impact of the project is considered critical to the company's strategy as articulated in the initiatives and vision. The project champion can often smooth the path of the project team in terms of getting resources allocated to the process from various parts of the organization. Project supporters come from key stakeholding areas of the business. These are the areas that may be affected by the project.

IT managers' roles

IT managers play the following roles:

- project coordinator
- technology manager
- communicator.

Project coordinator

A person who works with the project owner to coordinate the resources required for the project and to give a technology perspective to the whole process.

Technology manager

A person who keeps the project team aware of the technological implications of actions and manages the technology resources. These will be integrated with business and organizational concerns.

Communicator

A person working with human resources representatives and business managers to ensure that the organization understands the importance and nature of the project, and that the appropriate mechanisms are in place to assist business people learning how to use the IT. A good rule of thumb is that IT managers should never be project owners of business systems projects. The project owner may also select a project manager to manage the project on a day-to-day basis. This person can come from either the business or the IT side.

By understanding the roles of managers on projects, companies will know who controls IT spending in their business. Once the roles for a project are defined, the next step is to understand the importance of the investment.

Discounted cash flow (DCF) and net present value (NPV)

These are accounting techniques which are explained in *An Introduction to Operations Management* by C.D.J. Waters, Addison-Wesley, England, 1991.

Incomes which are generated at different times can be compared by discounting amounts to their value at the same point in time. The same discounting could be done for costs. The usual convention is to find the

continues

continued

equivalent present values of all costs and incomes. Then, subtracting the present value of all costs from the present value of all incomes gives a 'net present value'.

If the net present value is negative a product will make a loss and should not be introduced. If several alternative products have a positive net present value, the best one is the one with the highest value. A company selects a discounting rate by taking into account interest rates, inflation, taxes, opportunity costs, exchange rates and everything else. The discounting rate which gives a net present value of zero is called 'the internal rate of return'.

How much should be spent?

The first priority is to know what the company is currently spending. Unfortunately many companies do not have an accurate idea of this. The usual practice is to count the amount of money spent by the IT department. However, less than 50% of IT investment is actually controlled by formal IT departments. The increasing use of microbased technology in the form of PCs and workstations allows business users to take more of the management control and responsibility for IT. In order to assess how much the company is spending and where, it must take into account IT bought throughout the organisation. Table 6.1 shows how much businesses are spending, on average, on IT by industry.

Table 6.1   Average IT spend by industry

	% total annual expenditure
Financial services	12.0
Computers	10.0
Banking	10.0
Utilities	7.0
Aerospace	6.0
Insurance	5.0
Transportation	4.5
Electronics	3.0
Health care	3.0
Recreation	3.0
Chemicals	2.5
Forest products and paper	2.0
Appliances	2.0
Automobiles	2.0
Broadcasting and publishing	2.0
Metals	1.5
Beverages	1.0
Food and household products	1.0
Real estate	1.0

As business managers take more control over the applications of IT in business areas, more of the spending controlled by the IT department is for infrastructure to 'glue together' non-controlled technology. Examples are:

- local area networks (LANs)
- networks to link PCs and workstations
- data repositories for PCs
- data management for organizations
- training for PC users.

LAN

A LAN (local area network) is a network that serves IT facilities throughout one location. A network linking personal computers in a bank would be referred to as a LAN. If a company has two physical locations joined by a network, this is called a connection of two LANs or a WAN (wide area network). Taken to a further level, a network that links many locations is simply called a network, and must either be carried by a private service network provider or by one of the utility companies offering this service.

Categories of spending need to be established. These are dependent on the stage of IT development and the company's strategic objectives. Spending should be roughly 25% for infrastructure, 15% for development and 60% for production and maintenance. Since most of the spending on a system occurs after the development phase to keep the system up-to-date and running, curbing production and maintenance budgets after a system has been developed may be detrimental. Cutting the maintenance budget has been the end of many a good system which has become obsolete before the investment has been recovered.

Once the level of spending has been established, managers can look at spending patterns over time. Companies cannot sustain over 30% compounded growth for more than a few years. At that rate it is not possible to absorb all the changes into the business. On the other hand, less than 10% growth will usually not allow the investment to keep up with the business over time; old systems die and new technologies need to be introduced and maintained.

In general, management should be spending more in the high priority areas of the business to align investment with business strategy. In most cases the most important areas of the business are those in which IT spending should be concentrated. Some companies make the mistake of controlling IT spending by limiting it to some percentage of revenue. The important test is how much revenue the IT system will help to generate when it is in place; for example, for every £1 spent, £3 revenue will be generated. Thinking of IT spend in the context of return, or benefits planning, is a way of thinking about IT as a business asset rather than an expense item.

Cost/benefit analysis

It is estimated that the amount spent on computers worldwide is around $300–400 bn. These figures are often based on those given by hardware, software and service companies, such as systems integrators, consulting firms and so on. There is, however, another significant cost that firms must consider: this is the cost of the time spent by members of the company in planning and implementing IT systems. This is referred to as the implicit cost of computing. The explicit cost of computing refers to all those costs normally associated with IT: hardware, software, IT personnel. In most leading firms making substantial use of IT, the explicit cost is 3–9%, depending on the industry. The implicit costs can add a significant percentage to the overall cost.

Dr Diane Wilson, a research affiliate of MIT's Sloan School of Management, stressed the importance of analysing investments considering both the implicit and explicit costs. Her research focused on the roles CEOs play in IT investment:

> In most companies it is too easy to justify investment in new hardware. More difficult is determining the changes in organizational structure, management quality and customer satisfaction that might result from an investment in new IT. These changes or transformations directly relate to the kinds of questions that top managers ask about IT effectiveness. Simply stated, there are three: (1) How well are we doing the things we are doing? (2) Are we doing the right things? (3) Are we fit to compete in the future?
>
> Unless the top IT executive has performance indicators for each of these three questions he or she runs the risk of not providing top management with the kind of assessment information they want. Generally top management want to understand the project in terms of indicators that measure performance against competitors' performance. This means that managers have to communicate about the project in terms of a set of performance measures that they think create leading practice.

If there are hidden costs, there are also hidden benefits. In many cases the development phase of a project is completed but the benefits of the system are not audited. This is a powerful omission.

Opportunity costs, both in terms of what it would cost the company in market share not to undertake the project and the costs of management spending time on IT rather than on their primary responsibility such as marketing to the customer, must also be assessed.

An important opportunity cost to include in the calculation is the time gained in completing tasks that would result if the necessary IT were in place. For example, Mast Industries Inc., a clothing manufacturer in Andover, Massachusetts, USA, has placed computer-aided design terminals in its buyers offices as well as in some of the production offices around the world. Alison Grudier, CAD department manager, explained: 'Previously we would have to send out the paintings of a design to our buyers and suppliers. At the very least, we would be using overnight couriers to deliver these packages. By connecting through our CAD network, we can save several days on every design we make.'

Measuring the benefits and costs of IT involves articulating the 'soft' costs and benefits as well as the hard, using financial measures based on the investment analysis method preferred by the company. Some examples of these methods are as follows.

- Return on investment expressed in terms of discounted cash flows (DCF) or net present value (NPV) that stresses the payback period
- Comparative performance expressed in terms of market share, cost restructuring, or new products introduced *vis-à-vis* competitors
- Value analysis expressed in terms of how the project affects the operation and culture of the business.

Whichever method or combination of methods the company uses, two important factors must be taken into account: the term or length of the investment and when the return is expected; and the inclusion of all tangible and intangible organizational considerations.

The length of the investment is an important consideration. A system provides benefits of varying value over time. Similarly, costs vary over the life of the system. Most of the cost of the system, some 60%, will be in keeping it running and in the maintenance and enhancement that takes place after development. Many companies err by including only the development costs in appraising the system.

Organizational factors include those that affect the power of the business people to do their jobs, such as:

- the ease of use of the system
- the increased technology skills built by the system
- the level of business knowledge embedded in the systems that can be transferred to any employee in the network
- the added communication that enhances the corporate culture.

Successful investment in IT depends on managements' perspective on the multidimensional effect of the system and the dynamics of the marketplace. Simple cost/benefit analysis of the hardware system will not suffice. One CIO gave an example:

I know of a mail order business that did a cost/benefit analysis on the IT system it wanted to implement. The management of the company tried to find the lowest cost system to contact its customers in the cheapest way. This turned out to be a system which issued mail order letters to attract customers. The result was that it lost customers. The cheaper letters were not effective. The company had to move to motivate customers to help provide effective data entry. In the company's target market, no one likes to write letters any more. They have all moved from mail order to telephone order. The company rethought its approach to the market and decided to use the systems to provide market segmentation information to telesales people so that they had the most up-to-date information on the customer. In the end the approach was not the cheapest, but it was the most effective.

Some business managers are under the misapprehension that they cannot be involved in the IT investment analysis process. As one business manager said: 'The experts control the money in the sense that only the IT people really know what the investment is.' This is not true. If costs and benefits are not understood by business managers, then investment in IT becomes a bottomless pit for the company's resources. Business managers who depend too much on IT people to communicate about investment decisions are increasing the financial risk of the company.

Planning projects in order of priority

All the major stakeholders should be involved in assessing the priority of investments in IT in order to develop a healthy portfolio of projects. This team decides the strategic necessity of the projects, how they relate to the existing portfolio, and how the portfolio can be leveraged for the future.

A balance of quick strike and longer-term benefits should be sought in the investment programme. Business users of the system are generally impatient. They want to see some form of pay-off as the system develops rather than wait for a great balloon of benefits at the end of the project, perhaps years in the future.

The risks should also be balanced. Some projects will represent backbone systems which the company relies upon on a day-to-day basis. These systems may be well structured, governed by formal systems development methodologies. Other projects will represent new ventures the company hopes will pay off in the future. A venture management approach should be taken with radical change projects; management should expect to lose as many as they win. The management structure will be less formal than in the traditional projects.

Risk is controlled by considering:

- the size of the project
- the structure of the project – its complexity, number of units involved and so on
- the technology – how new it is, the team involved

- organizational change management issues – culture, adaptation to new technology, integration with the way things are currently done and the way people hope to do things in the future.

The portfolio should carry systems that are in different phases of their lifecycles – birth, growth, maturity and decline. The progress of projects and their relationship to other projects can be monitored by setting up timetables of objectives to be reached at periodic intervals. All projects should have a chart defining the roles and responsibilities of business and IT managers. Project-steering committees with representatives from all stakeholder areas can act as a key control mechanism involving multidisciplinary teams.

How to ensure a positive return on investment

It is most important for managers to be involved in the process. If management do not specify the benefits they expect, then they have no right to complain about the results they will invariably get. Some systems actually increase costs and produce negative benefits. Management can pull the plug out more easily if they understand how the system has fallen short of its objectives, and what effort it will take to create a new project to achieve the desired effect.

The objectives of all projects should be specified at the outset. Timeframes should be stipulated for benefits. New ventures as well as traditional projects should be tied to the business strategy. Communication of the project's objective and how it will be achieved can provide exponential benefits. The secret of managing business IT is to coordinate the human effort throughout the organization so that everyone understands the objectives and is committed to taking part in the development and running of the project. As managers become more technologically literate they will start looking for opportunities to integrate IT with the business vision. In many cases technology's greatest antagonists become its greatest protagonists as they realize what dimensions IT can add to the business.

As the world moves into the information age, business executives and managers that learn to harness the power of IT will have a tremendous advantage. Managers who integrate their understanding of business with their understanding of IT will be able to:

- get closer to their customers by understanding customer preferences and purchase profiles
- achieve better time-to-market results by integrating design and manufacturing decisions and supporting service workers with knowledge-based systems
- become leading global players by focusing on where the business will be in the future.

Action checklist

(1)   Who controls IT spending in your company? Are there many stake-holders involved in both the business and IT areas of the business?

(2)   Does the IT investment leave room for change? How is your company ensuring the flexibility of the investment? What percentage of the investment accounts for infrastructure, such as networks and applications that support the whole business?

(3)   On project management teams, who is in charge? Is there a team of people involved? Is accountability clear? Are projects clearly linked to strategic objectives?

(4)   What are some of the intangible benefits of IT projects?

(5)   Which projects tend to get investment approval? Do these reflect the strategic areas of importance of the business?

(6)   How does the company's management decide which projects go first, second, third? Are priorities set with all the stakeholders involved?

7

The impact of IT on the organization

- The knowledge an organization makes use of information throughout the business.

- 'Systems thinking' is a way of viewing the business as one, holistic information mosaic.

- Companies are moving from a functional orientation to a process organization to take advantage of the strategic value of information flows in the business.

- Building a consistent management information flow helps to build a stable and flexible management process.

The knowledge organization

In 1597, Francis Bacon wrote, 'Nam et ipsa scienta potestas est,' (knowledge is power). In 1962, at a White House address honouring Nobel Prize winners, President John F. Kennedy said, 'in a time of turbulence and change, it is more true than ever that knowledge is power.' As we move from the industrial age to the information age, organizations will undergo turbulent change. The competitive rules for many industries are being changed by telecommunications and information science. Managing information, knowledge and change are important to the organization of the twenty-first century. The ability to connect information flows with customers, suppliers, and within the company to get information to people who need to know is of paramount importance.

For example, the field sales staff of insurance companies used to have to call back to head office to get details of services and combinations for policies to tailor insurance offerings to clients. For the insurance agent who visits a customer's home, this meant that the agent would visit the home, discuss the insurance offerings and needs with the potential client, put together an estimate of the cost of the policy and then leave to call head office. The agent would then have to have the policy approved before the customer would commit to purchase. Valuable time for the sales agent was lost. The customer would also have time to think over the purchase and change their mind.

Today, many insurance agents carry electronic notepads or micro-computers which can connect via modem to head office. The agent can select a configuration of product and service offerings with the customer on screen. The agent can then ask for approval while connected to head office. If additional information is required, the agent can obtain it from the customer. If the customer wants specific knowledge about an area, the knowledge of the organization can be made available through databases and access to specialists. The agent can conclude the sale in one visit.

If you look at any point-of-sale or delivery today, you will see companies attempting to build on-line data connections. Delivery couriers carry light pens with which to scan identification codes on the sides of packages so that the company has access to information about where the package is at any time the package is on route. Many courier companies offer to put on-line connections into the customer's offices so that the customer can query the system directly to trace the package throughout the delivery cycle.

Companies are trying new ways of doing business based on the connection of information flows within and outside of the company. The models for the twenty-first century organization are in the process of emerging. One fundamental difference between the models of the twentieth and the twenty-first century organizations is that information flows are treated differently. Information flows of the future will be free from many of the time and location constraints that dictated the rigid organization forms of the past.

We do not yet know what the model of the twenty-first century organization will look like. However, we do have a number of interesting clues from interesting thinkers who are approaching this topic. One fundamental idea that is playing a large part in the formation for the corporation of the future is 'systems thinking'. The idea is to view any business activity as a whole system of information, perception, values and activities. Peter Senge, director of the systems thinking and organizational learning program at MIT's Sloan School of Management, gave an excellent example of systems thinking:

> A cloud masses, the sky darkens, leaves twist upward and we know that it will rain. We also know that after the storm, the run-off will feed into groundwater miles away and the sky will grow clear by tomorrow. All these events are distant in time and space, and yet they are all connected within the same pattern. Each has an influence on the rest,

an influence that is usually hidden from view. You can only understand the system of a rainstorm by contemplating the whole, not any
individual part of the pattern.

Business and other human endeavours are also systems. They,
too, are bound by invisible fabrics of interrelated actions, which often
take years to fully play out their effects on each other. Since we are
part of that lacework ourselves, it's doubly hard to see the whole pattern of change. Instead, we tend to focus on snapshots of isolated parts
of the system, and wonder why our deepest problems never seem to
get solved. Systems thinking is a conceptual framework, a body of
knowledge and tools that has been developed over the past 50 years,
to make the full patterns clearer, and to help us see how to change
them effectively.

Michael Porter summed up the effect of system's thinking on a firm's
strategy as: 'Corporate strategy is what makes the whole add up to more than
the sum of its unit parts' (Porter, 1987). Management control of information
flows can determine whether this holistic strategic value is achieved or not.

A pioneer of systems thinking, Jay Forrester described the essential role
information plays on the holistic character of the firm and management control,

The quality of management control depends upon what information
executives use and what they use it for, as well as on their skills as
administrators. As a system the company has certain characteristics
which are completely independent of individual functions or departments, just as an electronic computer has certain characteristics as a
system of parts. Without an awareness of basic information-flow
principles, it is only through costly error that managers can develop
an effective intuitive judgement (Forrester, 1958).

Information flow is fundamental to the successful management of the firm.
As new information technologies allow the integration of microprocessing,
with interactive media of sound, text and video, and access to databases, a
revolution in the way people work together to build the success of the organization is occurring.

The move from functional to process organizations

As we move from the industrial age to the information age, we are moving from
a functional orientation of business to a process orientation. In the hierarchical
organization, managers and workers possess and hold knowledge about a
particular functional aspect of the business, for example, design, marketing,

manufacturing, delivery or customer service. The goal of each functional department is to achieve performance targets set within the function. Design will attempt to introduce interesting products, marketing will attempt to record a high number of sales; manufacturing seeks to create products in a low-cost, efficient manner; distribution attempts to deliver products and services to retail outlets quickly and effectively; and customer service resolves customer complaints and queries.

In the process organization, the entire company focuses on achieving processes that run across the organization, such as achieving high customer satisfaction, becoming more global, or restructuring the cost-base of the company.

Case 7.1   *National Westminster Bank ServiceLine*

Context

This organization is attempting to move from function to process by creating a service process within the bank itself. As technology increases NatWest's ability to service the customer, the bank has developed a system called Service-Line to help branch banks as quickly as possible with their technology queries.

Why change?

Peter Holton, Manager of ServiceLine, described the system.

> The purpose of ServiceLine is to provide one number to staff at the branches, the users of our services, to call to help solve technology issues. The need for ServiceLine came out of the increasing dependence of branches on technology. For example, if an ATM goes down, the branches don't have staff to hand out money. In the bank's drive for customer service, we focused on IT on providing a service. Much of the technology at our branches should be available 24 hours a day or performs critical tasks such as balancing the day's work at the end of every day.
>
> Before ServiceLine, we had a lot of disparate help desks around answering questions on branch hardware, networking and connectivity, or on procedural queries about how to use technology. Bringing these services together helps us to provide a better service in less time.

continues

continued

The way it works

The system is a knowledge system that was developed with IBM. The moment a query is logged, that incident is recorded by the system. Possible solutions to the problem are offered to the service representative talking to the branch. If the problem goes beyond the knowledge of the system and the people involved, an expert such as an engineer is called to go to the site of the problem.

In terms of management information, we can see how the technology in the branches is performing, as well as problems and how they are resolved. We build incident records of the problems and solutions and work on those. The system provides a level of consistency across the company. ServiceLine allows us to take ownership of the technology issue to allow the branches to go back to work. We own and manage the technology faults.

The nature of work is changing from the original concept. Employees are empowered to improve the process and are provided with consistent guidelines and scripts to back them up. We count on the ServiceLine people to provide a professional response to the branches, take ownership of the call, manage the issue, and, if they can't clear the problem, to know a person who can.

The branch staff have different level of experiences with technology, so it is important to have a reliable human/machine system to help deal with technology issues. The interpersonal skills of ServiceLine representatives are the starting point. Learning how to work with the expert system is an art.

The future

Technology allows a flexible work staff to work flexible hours. The knowledge base is always updated. At the moment, we can handle 2000 calls per day, the bulk of which occur between 7 a.m. and 7 p.m., although we have people available 24 hours a day. The system contributes to the NatWest branch infrastructure capacity.

The benefit to the system has been that we can measure the performance of the technology in the branches. Since this technology is offered directly to the bank's customers in many cases, such as the ATMs, the measure of technology performance has a great deal to do with keeping customer satisfaction high.

Another benefit is that we generate a lot of management information about the technology we use. As soon as you have a single source of knowledge about the technology you buy, you can start negotiating very detailed contracts based on performance measures.

In the move to a process orientation, the manager's role is changing. Two researchers described this change:

> A manager's task may be compared to a movie director's. Viewed continuously and from a certain distance, the film appears seamless. Apparently the director's only challenge is to inspire the actors. But stage directors who become film directors learn that gestures that look subtle on the stage seem rather gross in the cutting-room. Once stage directors move to film, they have to think more like film editors. To control and integrate their product they have to understand the nuances, frame by frame.

Description	Functional manager	Process manager
Content relates to what managers are concerned about communicating with other managers from other functional areas as well as how they go about determining what should be communicated successfully or unsuccessfully.	What do I need to know?	and who else needs to know?
Currency relates to the timing of communication between managers from different functional areas as well as how managers go about determining whether information should be communicated and when information actually is communicated in a timely or untimely fashion.	When do I need to know and how current must the information be?	and when do other managers need to know?
Simultaneity relates to how managers consider decisions from two or more functional areas to be associated, how managers determine in what situations the interdependence of decisions affects management decisions, and how the decisions actually do occur interdependently either successfully or unsuccessfully.	What do I need to know and when?	and who else needs to know, and when, so that we can make related, coordinated decisions at the same time?
Cultural fit concerning management decision support relates to how managers communicate through the use of language to establish coherent methods of coordinating management decision-making toward common corporate goals.	Function-specific language and objectives	Consideration of translation of language and objectives across functional boundaries

Figure 7.1 The differing information concerns of functional and process managers. (*Source:* Daniels, 1992.)

Like film directors who master editing, manufacturing managers have to learn how to cut and splice small, discrete 'frames' of information, then build them up in more elegant, internally consistent ways. A manager who doesn't understand one part of a factory process as well as the other parts finds it impossible to make the necessary trade-offs between cost and smoothness, say, or speed and robustness (Hayes and Jaikumarr, 1988).

Information management needs differ between the functional and process organizations. The way managers think about information needs in the functional and process organizations differs. My research with companies has shown that functional managers have different information concerns than do process-oriented managers. These differences can be described with four concepts: content, currency, simultaneity and cultural fit. Figure 7.1 describes these concepts.

Content, currency, simultaneity and cultural fit

Content

The content of information requirements changes when an organization moves from a functional to a process perspective. The functional worker may only be concerned with what they need to know to carry out their tasks and make decisions. Structural differences from function to function can affect the ways management information is organized and effect the ways business process structures are organized.

To understand this more clearly, consider an example. In the clothing industry, many companies perform both the design and the manufacturing of garments. With increasing competition, clothing companies are trying to shorten the design to manufacturing to market cycle as well as more closely matching the products to consumer preferences. With the widespread use of electronic point-of-sale technology by clothing retailers, many companies have up-to-the-minute information about what customers are buying. The fashion business is a fast-paced industry.

With a functional orientation, each department completes its task before passing the product on to the next department. Design and marketing often work in tandem to produce a concept that the customer, the clothing retailer in this case, wants to buy. Once the customer has agreed to purchase a particular garment, the race begins.

In a functional organization, the design department passes the design to pre-production. Marketing, considering that the sale has been made, also passes the information about the garment to pre-production. Workers in design are measured on the number of designs they produce and the number that are accepted by the customer. Marketing workers are measured by the number of sales they contract with the customer and the margin between the sales price and the cost of making the goods. Information about the product is passed in a one-shot transmission. Anything from hastily noted specifications for the product to complete drawings, physical samples and mathematical calculations are passed through to the pre-production phase.

During pre-production, production workers convene to decide how the garment will be made with respect to materials used, time required to make and how the garments will be allocated to production lines and delivered to warehouses in time for the distribution department to plan delivery. Production workers are measured by their efficient use of time and materials. They may modify the original design to substitute materials that would contribute to cost savings or time savings. Sometimes these changes are communicated back to marketing and design but often they are not. When the goods are finished, they are passed to the distribution department. The distribution department is responsible for managing warehouse space, vehicles and timely delivery. Distribution workers are measured on the saving of time and cost of storage space.

This functional system works pretty well, and indeed it is a hallmark of the industrial age. With the information age, however, the competitive rules of the industry change. Clothing retailers increasingly want to minimize the return of unsellable products. They want to be the first in the market with the latest fashions. They also want to change their orders during the design to manufacturing to delivery cycle to take into account buying patterns learned during the buying season.

Complexity is introduced into the clothing manufacturer's business information management when communication across functions becomes continuous. Communication about product specifications from the customer no longer takes place on a one-shot basis, but is continuous. Management decisions are no longer discrete, but are now more interdependent. Figure 7.2 illustrates.

As managers make decisions about the product, in this case a garment, there is an effect on how other managers make decisions. For example, if the marketing manager and the customer agree that changes to the garment should occur, manufacturing and costing need access to that information to determine the best way to make the garment and how much the garment will cost to make. The content of the information about the product has to be communicated to each of the managers involved in the creating and making process. Whereas the functional manager need only be concerned with what they needed to know while performing their work, now they need be concerned with what other managers need to know. The content of information needs must be shared across the process.

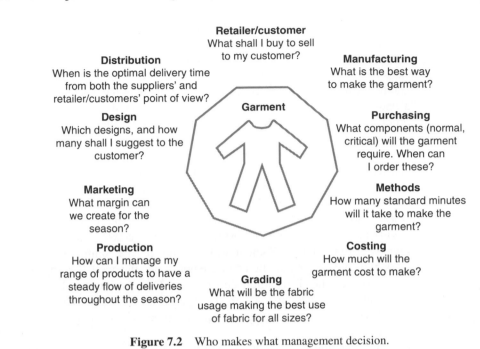

Figure 7.2 Who makes what management decision.

Currency

Similarly, the timing of the communication among managers must change. Instead of having a one-shot transmission of specifications, managers must determine how often they should communicate changes to other managers. For example, marketing may be discussing the possibility of changes with the customers on a frequent basis, but, perhaps, only when the changes have been finally agreed by the customer, are they then communicated to the rest of the company's managers. Different organizations will have different requirements for the currency of information, depending on how the employees work together.

Simultaneity

The process organization should make coordinated decisions. That is, many managers may simultaneously consider a given set of circumstances and share decision-making. Note that in this example, if any particular manager makes a decision, the product is changed. Thus, any particular decision has a dynamic effect on the product and on the decision-making process for the management team as a whole. Process managers consider the interdependencies of decisions, or how decisions are associated. Process managers determine in what situations one manager's decisions affect another manager's decisions, and how. In some instances, managers make decisions at the same time to ensure that the interdependent decision-making processes relate to each other. We call this the consideration of the need for making simultaneous decisions.

In moving to a process organization, trouble arises because of the different orientation in the way departments structure their activities and work. For example, departments may have a high or low degree of structure, be market- or product-focused, or have a way of working with people either permissively or dictatorially. Lorsch and Lawrence (1965) called this the 'organizational paradox' that the need for integrating specialized functions creates. That is, while companies must specialize to fulfil different functions such as design, marketing and production, there is a high need of coordination across activities to achieve effective innovation and process management.

Cultural fit

In a functional organization, different parts of the organization have specific vocabularies they use to communicate about specialized activities. This language is then transferred to more general situations. For example, the concept of 'product cost' is an important concept right across the organization. To a large extent, the company's margin and survival is determined by product cost. However, few large functional companies have a shared idea of what 'product cost' refers to across the functional activities. Marketing managers describe the elements of a product cost from their perspective, manufacturing managers from their's. Their different definitions are dependent on how their performance is measured. The marketing manager believes the 'product cost' is the amount determined with the customer that the company will spend for production of the product. The manufacturing manager believes the 'product cost' is the actual cost of making the garment. Only when all managers throughout the process are measured on what a shared concept of 'product cost' is – the cost of producing a product that has been delivered to the customer – will managers attempt to define a common language across the processes of the organization.

Managers working in a process-oriented organization have a shared idea of what content, currency, simultaneity and cultural fit characteristics their communications and information flows need throughout the company. In this way, managers and knowledge workers build a capability to have a stable but flexible management process with the ability to change product and service offerings on a dynamic basis.

Management View 6

Steve Collins, Director and Vice President, World Financial Systems, SmithKline Beecham

SmithKline Beecham is one of the world's leading health care companies. It discovers, develops, manufactures, and markets human and animal pharmaceuticals, over-the-counter medicines, consumer health care products and clinical laboratory testing services. Represented in over 130 countries, in 1992 sales turnover reached £5.2 bn. The company currently has 54,000 employees worldwide.

SmithKline Beecham has grown by acquisition with the major merger occurring between SmithKline and Beecham in 1989. Steve Collins, director and vice-president of World Financial Systems, has championed an approach to help move SmithKline Beecham from a functionally oriented company to a process-oriented company.

Steve Collins described the way management tackled the issue:

In 1989, due to our merger of two equal companies in the pharmaceuticals industry, we recognized that we had a need to revise our business systems and procedures. We noticed that we had a problem in intercompany accounting. Most companies have the same problem of integrating accounts over a number of operating companies. We looked at solving the problem with a business partner who we thought understood the complexities SmithKline Beecham was facing. The attraction of working with the IBM Consulting Group is that IBM had been through a similar project and we felt they could tackle it with experience.

Pharmaceutical companies have massive intercompany accounting issues since we do research in some locations, produce in others, and ship all over the world. Once we got into looking at the issues and the business processes associated with intercompany accounting, we realized that what we were looking at was not just an accounting problem but also a logistics, order, shipping and stocking problem. In fact, what we had was a business process and information flow problem that covered our whole supply chain to our customers.

We enlarged the scope of the project. We began to tackle the issue of what common systems our companies should have and what sort of communications systems we should have. What started as an intercompany accounting problem flushed out all sorts of intercompany process problems. We decided we had to improve our information flow between the plants and between the plants and the corporate holding company. We decided that now is the time since SmithKline Beecham is transforming from a holding company to a globally integrated company and without having integrated information flows, no company can successfully make this transition.

continues

continued

The group finance director, Hugh Collum, gave us the one essential ingredient for the project-organizational support. He empowered us to go ahead with the project. We identified the project as a 'Breakthrough' project, as part of our 'Simply Better Way' programme that identifies priority projects in the company. This project is a culture and business process project of finance and logistics.

By identifying projects as breakthroughs, we can build the organization of tomorrow without waiting for long strategic projects to give us the future direction. We had to work with the frailties of the existing systems while building the infrastructure of the future. We had a working model in a few months and a formal project soon after that.

SmithKline Beecham's CIO, John Parker, also ensured that the project was led from the top. We communicated the big picture of changing our company to a global integration of communications to down to the plant level.

The benefits to the company are: reduced stocks, a reduced cycle time and a reliable communications and process infrastructure. In the future, we hope to electronically trigger all shipping, ordering, manufacturing and delivery throughout the SmithKline Beecham supply chain to our customers.

Most important in succeeding in a project of this nature is to:

(1)   have a strong strategy that will allow the project to sail through the turbulent waters of strategic and organizational change. Don't let the project be schedule driven, make it business process driven. In a business process redesign project, the essential activities are: (a) define what the business process ought to be; (b) visit a representative cross section of the company to ensure that the design is of high quality; (c) define how to get to the new business process from the present approach. To really make changes, you have to do something different. At SmithKline Beecham, this project was not just about accounting, it was to build a business process that has no functional barriers

(2)   have strong leadership with total backing from above; be empowered for project and be given the authority to carry it out

(3)   break the whole project into prioritized projects in an integrated way. The project must be: rigorous, defensible, reliable and repeatable. You have to look at the dependencies and cross-points to determine the interdependent processes. Do the project in the context of the big picture

(4)   put the best people on the project full-time; choosing the star performers sends a message throughout the organization. The

continues

continued

team should be multifunctional including both business and IT managers; but business managers have to take the lead. We do a lot of personal briefings with everyone involved. Letting people see the big picture is important because people will suffer before gains are made. Outgoing, communicative people that are good at handling social relations are important to the success of the project

(5) visit every site that will be affected during the design phase. To keep the project alive, everyone has to be informed about the initiatives. You can't just send documents out about the projects and assume people will read them. Individual questions and concerns come out during the visits that are important to the design of the project. Communicating one-on-one is key to ensure a strong design, implementation and feedback cycle

(6) create a two- or three-pilot model environment where people have a good setup so that the pilot can become a centre of excellence

(7) have a good relationship with suppliers

(8) have a quality (and short) implementation plan with an efficient roll-out that can produce benefits quickly

(9) quantify the benefits in terms of finance, organization and time. We had a payback in less than two years. Any project that lasts five years is doomed. There are a lot of intangibles. For example, how do you value reliable data and a visible process that is understood by the organization? These benefits allow the company to run more effectively in terms of people, time and money at the bank. Cycle time is probably the easy benefit to quantify

(10) perform quality checks on local implementation procedures to gather plenty of feedback for opportunities for continuous improvement. Audit down-stream feedbacks.

Business process redesign is essential to our business vision.

Action checklist

(1) How is knowledge used in your company? Is it built up into information knowledge structures for use?

(2) Are there information barriers in the company that prevent a smooth flow of activities?

(3)   Does your company have a functional or process orientation?

(4)   Does your organization use information to make the management process flexible?

References

Daniels, N. C. (1992). Bridging the gap: the use of information systems to shorten the design to manufacturing cycle in the UK clothing industry. Doctoral Thesis, London Business School: April

Forrester, J. W. (1958). Industrial dynamics: a breakthrough for decision makers. *Harvard Business Review*, 37–66, July–August

Hayes, R. J. and Jaikumarr, R. (1988). Manufacturing crisis: new technologies, obsolete organizations. *Harvard Business Review*, September–October

Lorsch, P. R. and Lawrence, J. W. (1965). Organizing for product innovation. *Harvard Business Review*, 109–22, January–February

Porter, M. E. (1987). From competitive strategy to corporate strategy. *Harvard Business Review*, 43–59, May–June

8

Implementing an IT strategy

- Implementing an IT strategy requires a new management perspective: understanding people's roles in terms of information processes.
- Implementation is closely linked to education and training in most companies; few employees know a great deal about it.
- It is critical to give employees a genuine role in creating new working practices, or they will reject the IT system.
- IT specialists should be closely involved in all business process discussions; only they can finetune the system to take account of important nuances in business practice. In this way the IT system is tightly integrated into the culture: the way business is done.
- Keep people fully informed about the timing of different stages of implementation.
- Recognize and encourage 'hybrid' managers: those with good business and technical skills.
- There is a critical shortage of good IT-skilled staff.
- Monitor the supply and demand of IT in the company; it changes fast as people learn.
- Do not just automate processes; technology for its own sake is not cost effective.
- Provide means of channelling the learning process and new business ideas arising from it. Provide adequate training and development.
- Bring in specialist outside services if necessary; this is probably cheaper than developing in-house capability, particularly for training purposes.

Implementing a business information architecture requires a great deal of management coordination. People from many parts of the company will be required to give their views about the system development. Business and IT managers need to know how to manage their resources in the new IT effort.

'The people part of IT, the roles and responsibilities of the various players, is the crucial link between having a vision and building a successful IT architecture,' explained Philip Langsdale, director of planning at Midland Bank. Most business and IT managers interviewed for this report agreed; they also agreed that this is where management is weakest.

Developing the information management skill in an organization involves pulling together a great many people both inside and outside the organization. It may mean talking with customers, suppliers and business partners to get their views about the information processes.

Managers need to understand the fundamentals of managing the new IT effort, which are:

- creating the new management agenda
- acting in the new management roles
- managing and organizing for change
- educating and training
- managing external support.

The roles given to business and IT managers throughout the project require a new management perspective. While managing and organizing for change, managers need to understand the relevant timing points for change and the principal of 'freeze, unfreeze, freeze'.

- Freeze: determining the point of view managers currently have about IT.
- Unfreeze: changing management's viewpoint about IT and the role IT plays in carrying out strategically important activities in day-to-day business.
- Freeze: educating managers about the role of IT and their continuing responsibility to ensure that IT plays the proper role in business.

Education and training play an important role in communicating the designs and purposes of the business information architecture. They help managers 'pass the torch' to the rest of the organization.

At times the company will have insufficient resources to manage the IT effort. Management may decide not to organize all the effort in-house since the expertise is too expensive to develop and outside companies are able to provide the service. Companies are increasingly turning to outside service providers as the complexity of IT escalates. Managers need to know how to manage both in-house and external resources.

Throughout the management of the IT process it is important to bear in mind the company's culture. Building on the strengths of the culture allows management to communicate the pros and cons of projects more effectively, knitting the business IT architecture into the fabric of the organization.

Creating the new management agenda

Keep up the momentum

Once the business information architecture has been spelled out in terms of projects and strategic initiatives, it is important to keep up the momentum of the overall effort. Entering at the implementation stage can give some employees the feeling that all the decisions have been made and only the tedious bits remain to be done, which is why they have been called in. Overcoming this attitude is a major challenge.

By highlighting the decisions that have not been made and describing the directions determined by the previous efforts, managers can point out that the heart of the project is yet to be accomplished. Involving these managers in assessing how the business processes work now and how they will work in the future will allow the business people to describe what the business systems will have to do and enable them to become more deeply committed to the process.

Get key people involved

The major task in the first phase of implementation is to spell out how the business processes operate today, how they will operate tomorrow and the factors that can eliminate the distance between them. By analysing the role of IT, the people involved in the implementation can see at first hand the reasons for using IT to help restructure the business processes. They will also determine the organizational changes needed to take the company forward. Once people understand that they are determining the company's future business practices and that the process requires their expertise, commitment will be high; participants like to be actively involved in new projects.

Another important task in the first phase of implementation is to pull as many key managers in the organization as possible into the project. They will then start to understand it from the inside and to build the roots of the longer-term support that will be needed as the systems begin to be engaged.

The IT people can gain an enormous amount from being involved in the business process discussions. They learn first hand the content and subtleties of the business processes. The subleties are important to catch. They can signify the success or failure of a project. It is often the nuances of the way a business process is carried out that generate its special value and the information that is available.

Construct a model

The depiction of how the business process will be carried out should culminate in a model, together with the information flows needed. A high-level prototype of the IT system to achieve this information flow can then be created by the IT people to illustrate the first attempt at automating the procedures.

The prototype is a useful tool for business people to play with. They can discuss what they like and dislike about the system to reinforce what the purposes of the business process and IT system are, how they intertwine and what the particulars of the system (such as the features for input, processing requirements and output) need to be. The prototype can also be shown to other people in the organization to begin to communicate the purposes of the project, as long as the audience understands that it is only a prototype. It demonstrates the directions that will be taken as a result of the project. This is the phase at which a project becomes real to many people in the company. A prototype answers the question, 'Just what have they been doing?'

There is a danger: people may begin to think that full implementation will take place sooner than it actually will. The business and IT managers should work together to develop a realistic timetable that describes the phased implementation of the process and system. The timetable will have three phases: prototype development; system development and initial implementation; and full implementation. It should be available to anyone who communicates about the project through the formal communication systems.

Criteria for success

The criteria for the success of the new management agenda are clear: the degree to which the organization adopts the project; how managers build support and momentum; and how they involve people in the project. A manager experienced with IT projects explained:

> The organizational aspects of implementation should focus on managing the business area's effort in the project and showing how IT can influence the organization of the company. This is vital. The new possibilities are important. Showing how the information flows can combine resources illustrates the organizational changes possible with IT. Today business users know more about IT in the business.

The new management roles

The business manager's role

Business managers' understanding of IT and IT managers' understanding of business processes vary.

- 'At SAS the business managers are learning. We have an advantage because our business is technology-driven. The charisma of the airplane makes technology attractive. We say we have to know how to "fly people" now,' said Bjorn Boldt-Christmas, director of strategies.
- 'At Midland Bank every manager is required to take a course. Our managers are computer literate,' said Philip Langsdale, director of planning.
- 'Business managers have problems with IT. Their major problem is not having time to understand what's possible. There is a gap between people who know and people who don't have time to appreciate what's possible. That's why the technology really should be user-friendly, so that it doesn't take much time to learn how to use it,' said Caroline Raby, head of marketing communications at Mercury Communications. 'People in business often don't realize what IT tools are available to help them. They would like to know, but the effort required to learn from available sources is greater than is acceptable to most managers.'

In every company the call to action by being supportive and involved in the business IT architecture must come from senior business executives and managers. Business managers are motivated to use IT on their own initiative by the recognition that a lack of understanding could block their development as managers.

Time is of increasing importance to managers. A critical factor in determining the value of IT for business managers will be whether it helps them to do things in a new way, and in a way that saves time.

New managers should have business and technology acumen. They need to be 'hard' diplomats in that they are willing to be flexible and include the use of IT in the job, yet firm in ensuring that the IT systems serve the business and not vice versa. Managers need to be technologically comfortable and to treat other business information users as cooperatives. By becoming more technologically literate, they become increasingly opportunistic about the use of IT.

Professor Michael Earl of the London Business School called business managers who understand the application of technology to their business 'hybrid' managers (1989). Hybrids can act as a bridge between IT and business managers who do not have significant expertise in each other's areas.

'Hybrids' has become a contemporary description for people with strong technical skills and adequate business knowledge, or vice versa

... Hybrids are people with technical skills able to work in user areas doing a line or functional job, but adept at developing and implementing IT application ideas.

The IT manager's role

One of the biggest worries in IT departments is that skilled staff are getting more and more scarce. Fraser Mitchell, head of the National Computer Company in the UK, described the problem in one company to Dr Alan Cane of the *Financial Times* (1990):

> UK companies are short of 19,300 computer specialists, about 11 per cent of the total 175,000 computer experts working for British companies, according to a survey by the National Computing Centre (NCC). The survey by NCC, the organisation charged with developing the UK's commercial computing potential, covers only computer specialists working for users of computers; it does not take into account specialists working for software houses or computer manufacturers. A shortage of experienced programmers and systems analysts has often been blamed for slow progress by UK companies in developing advanced computer systems. The NCC survey shows that the greatest shortage is of programmers, software specialists who write computer code. Analyst programmers, who size up the information needs of a business and design an appropriate computer system, are almost as scarce.

Staff shortages are becoming a global problem. Some forward-thinking companies are planning to locate IT training and operations in attractive settings, such as the French Riviera, to lure top talent. The shortages, however, are likely to grow.

Another problem is described by an exasperated senior executive: 'IT divisions are self-supporting and self-oriented. They know little about the company. They have created their own *raison d'être* and are quite absorbed with it. They keep too separate from the rest of the company.' The lack of hybrid skills among IT managers is a problem that can inhibit a company's ability to use IT. Henry Mintzberg is concerned that, as a result, IT managers will push technology solutions on to the business (see Management View 7).

It is necessary to establish partnerships between IT and business managers to use the full force of IT in the business. To generate the 'business pull' so that business needs drive the technology, IT managers need to be informed about the technology and the business processes, and to be good listeners and interpreters of business needs. The most important role for the IT manager is that of communicator.

The IT manager needs a sound understanding of the capabilities and realities of the technologies. Keeping abreast of new technologies is a massive job.

IT managers need access to outside sources of information to keep the business up-to-date with developments and, also, laboratories within the company to test the new technologies.

There needs to be an understanding of the organizational implications of using IT throughout the IT department. To integrate IT into business processes and to teach the organization to adapt to its use, IT managers need to have an understanding of the dynamics of organizational change. Business processes are restructured using IT. IT managers who understand the process of organizational change can anticipate the reactions of business users. The IT department can provide an example by looking at the potential for better management of its own organization through the use of IT.

Managing and organizing for change

The most effective implementations of business IT occur within a programme of planned change. Every application of IT changes the way work is done. Some changes are extensive, such as computer-aided design which allows designers to work in three dimensions, a new planning system that indicates where product is in the pipeline, or order processing systems linked to customers. In the increasingly global business environment, managing information plays a pivotal role. IT is changing the function of every job. The need to assess skills and develop a competent set of managers who are business and IT literate is becoming essential.

Balancing supply and demand: evaluating the IT skill base

In order to assess the skill base in a company an evaluation must be made of the experience of the business and IT people with respect to its present and future technology requirements. The assessment begins with the question: what is the current state of IT and the skill base within the business community?

Building the technological skills of business managers depends on how much experience they already have of using computers, of participating in or leading projects in the company, or of playing a part in customers' or suppliers' IT projects. Many business managers have taken IT courses as part of their formal training at school or have increased their knowledge from interest. Having a tally of the skills available identifies which people can be used in which projects.

Management View 7
Professor Henry Mintzberg

Managing involves different things. The issue is not that managers should use available technology but to find out what managers do and how they work. If they happen to need technology, that is fine. There has to be a pull, a need for business managers to use IT as a tool, not a push from IT managers saying, 'We have this great new machine and managers have to use it.'

I am concerned about the rule of the tool, the machine running around looking for places to be applied. Management is a natural process and people will use technology where it is relevant. The last people in the world who can tell them how to use it are the people who are enamoured with the machines. IT has got to be a draw rather than a push.

There is a lot of nonsense in this field. IT people are going to have to settle down to look at what is really going on and not to be so enamoured with glitzy machinery.

Managers collect everything from impressions, moods and gossip to very hard data. They get information through all kinds of channels and in all kinds of ways, some of which happen to lend themselves to machine processing, and a lot which do not. If a computer system is running and functioning well, then why would managers not use it as another vehicle by which they are informed?

If you are looking at the hours in a managerial week, there will be some hours when they tap into computers because the computer is useful for the organization. It is a channel of information but there are many others: one is to call around the board of directors to get their view on something, another is newspapers, another is magazines, another is the internal information systems. Fifty years ago they did not have computers; they read the accounting reports.

Any useful information that exists in an organization will inevitably get used one way or another by its management. They use everything they can get and obviously a lot of information is going to go through computers. That is not to say that management functions through computers. It is a very, very different concept.

Managers do almost the same thing that everyone else does, they just do not do it very regularly. If there is a scheduling system in place, occasionally a manager will intervene to find out what is going on, tapping into the system for one reason or another.

I am concerned about technology driving out intuition, and other human skills. We are not going to get rid of computers and I do not think any manager can function without access to a computer. But managers will treat IT as just another tool that is helpful, not the answer to everything. If managers want to understand business, they have to see through all lenses.

Matching the current state of skills with the desired state will also identify how much the IT department has to learn or acquire to produce a necessary skill base. Having an accurate idea of the technology skills and strengths helps to prevent companies from taking on too much or having unrealistic expectations of their systems departments. In addition to inside sources of IT skills, the capabilities of outside vendors to manage IT is important.

The profile of the company's IT skills should include:

- levels of staff skills and knowledge
- particular technology-related experience
- communication skills
- management skills.

Accurate descriptions of what skills exist and are needed provide the supply side of the IT equation with tangible parameters.

Since IT skills are becoming more scarce, considering what people are learning or should learn is of increasing importance. A profile of experience across the company should include:

- expected compensation levels
- career development plans
- performance management techniques
- headcount levels of both IT personnel and business users.

It is important to measure the level of expertise and business users' attitudes towards IT.

Cultivating IT opportunities

Management's ability to spot opportunities for developing IT will depend on their experience and understanding of the capability of IT. The most important point to deal with is management's understanding – it will place the company appropriately on the learning curve of IT.

The competitive progression of IT skills in a company is a useful trend to watch. Skills progress with each stage in a company's growth. In banking, as IT plays an increasing role in marketing activities, service representatives have learned how to access complex knowledge bases about products to help customers with financial planning. The representatives operate interactive systems with customers to help them 'try out' products to gauge the effect on their overall financial portfolio.

Not everyone agrees that IT produces the benefits that many businesses hope for. Lester Thurow, an economist at the Massachusetts Institute of Technology, believed productivity improvements brought about by the use of IT have not always been realized because businesses have failed to take into account the ability of IT to change the way work is done:

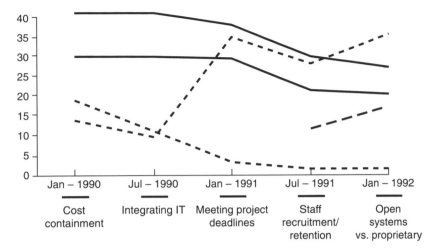

Figure 8.1   The top five issues for IT managers. (*Source:* Price Waterhouse/Computing Opinion Surveys. *Information technology Review* 1992–93.)

To computerise the office, you have to reinvent the office in terms of who reports to whom, what reports are generated, all those kinds of things. But ripping up the office and inventing a new office is socio-logically very difficult because you interfere with power arrange-ments, and you interfere with established customs and procedures ... [Increasing productivity with IT] really requires structural changes in the way we do things. Each bit of data is so cheap that we tend to gen-erate millions of bits, and then it ends up being horribly expensive. Thinking seriously about what we need and what we don't need – with the emphasis on what we don't need – is the way to go, because clearly you can do remarkable things with this technology. The ques-tion is how to keep it from burning up resources when it isn't doing remarkable things ... I think the bottom line has to be that you come at it with a focus on productivity rather than a focus on generating information (Thurow, 1989).

When designing IT systems it is important to focus on productivity and the commercial strategy of the company. To implement IT effectively, manage-ment must begin by taking into account the capabilities of IT for redesigning the business process. Merely automating manual procedures does not achieve the full benefits of IT. Companies must integrate business and IT procedures.

Management View 8
Bruno Zuccharo Director of IT, Benetton

What does IT mean exactly? IT is more than just the identification of hardware and software. IT is the sum of knowledge, methods and techniques for using information in business.

Managing IT is like managing any other technology. It is not enough to buy the tools. You must also think about human resources, knowledge, management capacity and skills. The way you manage innovation in IT is the same way you manage innovation in other areas of the business.

The understanding between business and IT people depends on an understanding of IT capability. Business managers need to know the why and the when of the management of systems. The timing has to be right. In the formative stages of product development IT can play a creative role in helping to determine how to produce the product or service. Later on IT does not have to be problem- and solution-oriented. It becomes more situational, improving processes.

The essential part of managing IT to commercial advantage is to learn the timing with regard to locking yourself into new technology: management must maintain a balance by being not too early and not too late.

The business manager should not try to act as substitute for the IT manager. The role of the business manager is in evaluating the business impact and opportunities of information and playing a part in the evolution of the systems. Business managers need to think about what and how to develop new ways to do business with information.

There is an opportunity here to be very clever. IT does not always require a lot of investment, but it must be smartly implemented. Advantages come from implementing smart business ideas with the use of information. In most businesses IT is used to reduce staff or replace manual work, or it is embedded in production technology rather than used to implement smart ideas.

At Benetton we try to be clever, thinking about how to develop a new way to do business. To push the market to buy, Benetton must be able to assure a quick service to the market. If a retailer buys goods and can have delivery in five days, sales volume increases. He or she can react to the market much more appropriately. This is a very different way of doing business. We could not implement this without IT.

Our market is the entire world. Sending information around the world, passing information, enables Benetton to make and ship products anywhere within three days of receiving the order.

Cost containment has become the IT manager's chief concern, closely followed by integrating IT with the business. As downward economic pressures continue, IT managers are attempting to restructure their systems efforts to support the business. Open systems continue to gain attention, while staff recruitment declines as a management issue of importance.

It is important that business managers recognize that the benefits of IT are attained by restructuring work. To get value for money business managers must lead in managing systems (McCulloch, 1988). Business managers are stepped up to bat, as Andrew Rigby, finance director of paper company James River, put it: 'Today's managers and executives want, in effect, to be the drivers of the IT car, they don't want to be experts or mechanics, but they want to be able to travel and manoeuvre.'

However, management are not always equipped with the technological literacy to carry this out. In the USA firms have failed to capture the benefits of flexible manufacturing because they used the computer machinery to produce high quantity runs of a narrow range of products, reproducing outdated strategies. Japanese companies, in contrast, are using IT to produce a wider range of products with higher quality, expanding both the scope and the flexibility of their enterprise. Technological literacy – understanding what the technology can do – is of increasing importance (Feder, 1986).

Education and training

How much time should be spent on training? Different types of training – applied learning (in the context of the workplace), informal and formal – should be combined to form the basic skills business people need.

Applied learning

The most effective training involves applied learning. That is training that takes place within the context of the business manager's everyday activities. The crucial issue to address is the impact of IT on the way business managers carry out their jobs. Interactive training should be available on an *ad hoc* basis. This can be achieved by using the system to provide some of the training. Learning can be an individual activity. An effective approach is to allow managers to choose the time they devote to sharpening their skills.

Informal training

Informal education and training can be provided by peers, help-desks and user groups. Having access to people who know the system well is a part of knowledge-sharing that should increase the company's overall knowledge of its systems.

Peers that have an interest in developing knowledge can share their experience up to a point, but sooner or later a few people become the systems' experts. While this is a good step towards developing knowledge of IT for business users, companies cannot afford to stop the spread of knowledge there. These experts eventually become inundated with requests and can begin to act as IT specialists themselves, forsaking their other job responsibilities. Providing a range of knowledge-transfer sessions helps to spread learning more evenly.

Help-desks are either telephone or walk-in areas where technologists with an understanding of the business process and IT system are available to answer questions. For business users the advantage is that there is always a knowledgeable person available to address system issues. For technology people the advantage is that the technologist interacts first hand with users of the system and is involved in its frontline testing. The experience also gives managers ideas for enhancing systems or for designing future systems.

Formal training

Formal education addresses cultural, business process and technology questions. Considered in concert, formal education is useful to bring people up-to-date with new technologies and plans for the future and to build a standard level of expertise throughout the business. However, formal training should be followed up with other forms of training to ensure that the learning is applied. The retention rates of formal learning over time are surprisingly low. However, when reinforced with informal and applied learning, retention rates for the formal part of training double.

For IT people, education in the business processes, human communication skills and IT are required. To gain the respect of business people, IT managers need to have a thorough understanding of the strategic objectives, major business projects and important information flows. Time spent in business meetings discussing business priorities is well spent. The more familiar the IT person is with the day-to-day concerns of the business people, the more they can translate the business needs into systems.

Communication skills should be both formally and informally worked on. Outside facilitators are sometimes more successful at teaching IT people how to improve communication than inside personnel. It is easier for outsiders to deliver certain messages, and they can provide a wide range of business communication expertise.

Keeping up with leading-edge technology is a two-step process. Each technologist has a specialist area that will require training from outside sources at least once a year. Transferring that knowledge to other technologists to plan for the integration of technologies is the second step in the knowledge-transfer process. As technologies impact on each other, IT managers must plan how to integrate the effects in the business.

Perhaps a better question would be: how much time should business and IT managers be learning in their jobs? By increasing the amount of learning, knowledge-building and sharing that is integrated with carrying out tasks, the knowledge base of the company increases over time, pushing the company upwards on the learning curve of business IT.

Learning should be a continuous process, integrated with the activities involved in carrying out day-to-day work. Employees should receive at least one week per year of training on how to use IT, as well as several weeks of instruction on how IT can be used to enhance the capabilities of the business.

As we move to the information age, more and more IT facilities will be available to employees to train in their own time, using multimedia capabilities and training programs. One of the most important skills of the future is the ability to learn how to integrate IT into the business place.

Using external support

As technological advances in IT occur more quickly and have more wide-ranging effects in business, it becomes increasingly difficult to be able to keep abreast of all developments by using only in-house expertise. For certain projects it may not be cost-effective to hire an expert full-time and keep him or her on the staff.

The use of external support is increasing. Companies are moving towards having a network of hardware, software, service and training advisers that they rely on. Forming relationships with a few providers allows managers to keep abreast of changes in the marketplace and to tap into the expertise when the company needs it.

Some companies contract out (or 'outsource') whole chunks of IT-related work. Facilities management, a service whereby the service provider actually runs the whole data centre, is a rapidly growing field.

The major tenets of outsourcing are:

- to form a relationship with a few service providers to keep aware of overall market trends
- to examine which services are provided
- to allow the IT managers to compare the products available
- to analyse the match of supplier offerings and business needs.

Working with the IT managers ensures that providers are dealing with technologists who understand the technological aspects of the offering and can measure the providers' ability to deliver.

The important business decision to be made about outsourcing: what should be outsourced and what should be performed by employees? Many companies have identified the strategic aspects of computing: systems design and programming, perhaps network creation and vendor management, and have tended to keep these activities in-house. Other more commodity-like activities, such as software programming implementation or network management, have been successfully outsourced. The company receives a service at a fee while the IT supplier operates a number of facilities to capture economies of scale.

Outsourcing activities can reduce the IT expenditure, however, a careful analysis of the long-term effects of outsourcing should be undertaken in order to evaluate the full effect of outsourcing an activity. Many companies have found that a temporary improvement one year to the IT expenditure has had to be made up for in following years because the activity has become strategic. A general rule of thumb is to in-source any activity that relates to the firm's relationship with customers, with systems development or network control.

The benefit of outsourcing is that the technique allows the company to focus resources on strategic activities of the firm and to capture economies of scale in non-core activities.

Action checklist

(1) Are business managers integrated into the IT planning and implementation process by taking responsibility for projects?

(2) What is the skill mix of the company's managers? Is there experience with a broad base of technologies?

(3) Does the company have a number of hybrid managers?

(4) Are opportunities to use IT considered with a view to better structuring business processes?

(5) What education and training is available to business and IT managers? Is this followed up so that the effect of the training is retained? How is knowledge about IT increased?

(6) Are there opportunities to outsource some of the company's IT activities?

References

Cane, A. (1990). Survey discloses shortage of computer specialists, *Financial Times*, 24 September

Earl, M. (1989). *Management Strategies for Information Technology*. New York and London: Prentice-Hall, 205–6

Feder, B. J. (1986). Technology: new challenge in automation, *The New York Times*, 30 October. The article describes the research of Professor Ramchandran Jaikumar of the Harvard Business School on comparative methods of implementing flexible manufacturing methods

Ludlum, D. (1989). New methods needed to make IS pay off where it counts – the bottom line: an interview with MIT's Lester Thurow. *Computerworld*, Special Campus Edition on Computer Careers, **2** (1) 14–15, 31 October

McCulloch, R. (1988). Line managers being forced to take the lead in technology, *Globe & Mail*, Toronto, Ontario, Canada, 7 November

Mintzberg H. (1990). Personal communications, 23 November

9

The business manager's role in development

- Technology has become more accessible to many people in the firm.
- Involvement of managers is important at all levels of system design and implementation.
- 'Hybrid' managers blend business and technology skills.
- Hands-on training with IT allows people to learn more about how to integrate business and IT skills.
- Executive information systems provide a high-level view of the company's key performance indicators.

Taking the lead

In the early days of computing, technology specialists came from engineering backgrounds, they had their own language and culture and they dealt mainly with the design aspects of machines. Machine code, the electronic language understood by early computers, was just that: a code of electronic impulses that had little meaning to human beings. At that time, technologists needed to develop the fundamental machine code of computers to a kind of alphabet or basic vocabulary, called programming languages, with which they could work to create a set of instructions for the computer. Writing code in programming languages took a great deal of time and also required a translation into a human language so that human programmers could understand what the programming language was directing the computer to do.

As time goes on, programmers are getting tired of learning intricate computer programming languages and are building sophisticated computer systems that will understand instructions set out in languages more easily understood by people. The technology barriers formed by programming languages are diminishing because user interfaces are being developed that are easier for non-technologists to understand.

As technology barriers diminish, the technologist is more available to business managers to discuss the aims and objectives of the corporation. Technology constraints no longer solely dictate the communication patterns between business managers and technologists. Business and technology managers can spend more time addressing the business needs with flexible technology rather than focusing on intricate idiosyncrasies of particular systems. In part, the micro revolution has spurred this change.

Power in the hands of managers

As we have seen in earlier chapters, the microprocessor revolution has brought processing power to managers. What does that mean, exactly?

In the days of the mainframe, there were four main parts of a computer system: the input device, the processor, the storage device and the output device. The input device was a terminal that transferred input from the keyboard to the rest of the parts of the computer. You can think of this as a typewriter capable of sending messages to the processor, the storage devices or the output device. The processor unit is the part of the computer that actually carries out tasks such as adding numbers, changing databases or altering a document to reflect editorial changes. This is the 'brain' of the computer that actually carries out everything but input, output and storage. Storage devices are things that hold information on a variety of media. Your cassette recorder is a storage device. Similarly, storage devices for computers can be on magnetic tape, or disks. An output device is a printer. Finally, for one computer to transfer information to another, a network is used. A network is a set of electronic connections between computers that conveys information.

In the days of the mainframe, a person would enter information on a terminal and send the information to the central processing unit (CPU) where the CPU would perform whatever activity was requested and send information back to the terminal. Many people shared the access to the CPU so it could take some time before the CPU could process your request. While you were waiting for the CPU to process your request, you were placed in an electronic queue of all requests to the CPUs by all the computer users. You might have to wait a long time. As business areas need for computing developed, the frustration level of waiting to have reports generated or programs run grew rapidly.

In the mainframe days, another constraint for managers who wanted to use IT was the systems development time of the IT people in the organization. There was only so much person power available to write the programs for the mainframe to run. The programming needs of various departments vied with each other for scarce IT human resources as well as machine resources. Marketing and sales programs would compete with distribution programs for development time. Very quickly, department managers sought ways to jump the queues.

Budgets are priority driven. Once the IT budget was determined for a company, there would typically be a meeting to prioritize and 'vote' on which programs would be developed over the coming year. If your area's programs were given priority, IT resources would be directed your way; if not, you would have to wait another year. Programming backlogs escalated to hundreds of person-years of waiting requests.

Business people can be resourceful. Pent-up demand for IT resources caused a reaction something like, 'Alright then, we'll do it ourselves.' And that, exactly, is what departments sought to do.

The micro revolution

Microcomputers, also referred to as PCs or personal computers, have processing capability within the small computer. In other words, given a few programs such as a text processor, a spreadsheet and a database, managers could process their own information requests. This would take some learning on the part of the manager, to master the basic programming packages, but those who were motivated made the cognitive leap.

Another advantage was that the price of microcomputers was often well below the department manager's budget limit, so that the microcomputers could be bought as 'office equipment' without the powers that be realizing that departments had gone out to purchase their own processing power.

IT people were also interested in getting out from the backlog to move into areas where they could build programs that would enhance the business's competitive advantage. As systems addressed more of the needs of functional areas, the demand for IT people who understood the overall objectives of the business grew. For example, to build an effective customer database, the IT person has to understand what the business manager wants to know about the customer and why. Knowing why customer databases were being built helps the IT person to anticipate and perhaps suggest future uses and developments of customer information.

As businesses build increasing flexibility to respond to the market place, people working throughout the organization are being empowered to take actions and make decisions. The coordination of many areas of the business is vital to support this organizational enterprise. Both the centralized and decentralized areas of the business need to have access to information about the changing conditions of business activities to ensure that consistency exists throughout the organization.

Strategic information technology efforts can be combined in the organization to gain greater leverage. Consider the example that Nestlé's CIO, Jean Claude Dispaux, cited as an example in Figure 9.1. Here, a customer in France orders products manufactured in two other countries, the UK and Italy. The products are sent to a warehouse in Belgium and will be delivered to the customer warehouse in Nigeria.

Several important activities are taking place here. First, the company is attempting to integrate business activities so that economies of scale are generated: the products manufactured by various plants are stored in a common warehouse in Belgium so that other orders can be combined and shipped to customers in adjacent areas. Supporting this effort, several information systems that serve functional areas of the business are integrated to provide information about the overall process of ordering, making and shipping goods to customers.

A major customer in France places an order for products which are manufactured in the UK and Italy. Those products are shipped to a common warehouse in Belgium and will be delivered as a single cargo load to the customer warehouse in Nigeria.

This involves:

- Sales support (e.g. profitability)

- Planning (e.g. multi-manufactures, timing, capacity)

- Manufacturing (e.g. product specification)

- Distribution (e.g. cross-border shipments)

- Data definitions (e.g. pallet tags, bar coding)

- Invoicing (e.g. multi-lingual)

- Data exchange (e.g. EDI)

We can see from this example that functional richness of the applications is also a very important factor.

Figure 9.1   Integrated IT and business activities.

Each application or system generates information for the business system that supports these cross-functional activities, enabling the organization to act as a whole. The left hand, so to speak, is made to communicate with the right. This is a clever example that shows how information from many systems can be leveraged to create a 'whole that is greater than the sum of its parts'.

The sales support system renders information about each particular sale, aggregate sales, margins and profitability. The planning system provides information about the manufacturing, timing and capacity of the many manufacturing plants owned by the company. Manufacturing contributes information about product specifications. Distribution contributes information about cross-border shipments, delivery schedules and routes, warehouse availability and the times of expected receipt by customers. Invoicing provides a dissemination of information on a multilingual basis. Data exchange methods and data definitions are the media of data that allow the information to travel from one IT system to the next, serving the whole business system. Data definitions such as pallet tag and bar coding and electronic data interchange.

Viewed together, these systems give managers an holistic view of the activities of the business. By concentrating on the information flows through the business as well as the goods flows, business managers get a better understanding of how activities take place in the company.

Management View 9

John Wallace, General Manager, Information Technology, National Westminster Bank

As General Manager, Information Technology in NatWest, transaction processing is very important to me. I provide support to all the various units and markets in which NatWest operates. My primary role, however, is to support our UK branch business or the domestic banking arm as it used to be known. For a company of NatWest's size and complexity this is quite a challenge.

There are three basic functions which every retail bank undertakes: first, the promotion and selling of savings products. We offer a wide range of account types, where customers can invest any surplus funds they may have. Second, on the lending side, we provide a range of facilities from bridging short-term needs to major project finance. Third, is transaction processing.

We handle many types of transactions – be they cash, paper cheques and credits or plastic credit and debit cards. We also need to respond to requests for information and we act on instructions to deal in various markets.

continues

continued

Increasingly, more and more of these transactions are handled on-line, so that we can react to changes in the world's markets and provide up-to-date information to our customers.

Because we're handling people's finances, the reliability, integrity and security of our systems is essential. The sheer volume going through our payments' systems, and the value of it, makes this a must. We have over 2700 branches, 14.5 million accounts, 7 million customers or one in seven of the population. We undertake 20 million transactions every day.

For years, this has meant handling an ever-growing mountain of paper. But we are now, for the first time, seeing a levelling off of the volume of paper, or cheques, as electronic methods of payment become more prevalent. The direct debit is significantly helping to reduce the amount of paper in the banking system. People now prefer to arrange computerized direct debit to pay the quarterly gas or electronic bills, as opposed to remembering to issue a cheque. In broad figures, NatWest made some 250 million direct debit payments and 50 million standing order payments by computer during 1991.

NatWest has developed the largest single ATM network in the UK. We've got over 2000 through-the-wall machines and a further 800 rapid cash tills situated in bank lobbies. These machines now dispense over 70% of all personal cash withdrawals made from NatWest. Last year alone they dispensed £6.7 billion, or £10,000 every minute of every day. Figures for 1992 show this has now risen to £12,000 every minute – a 20% increase.

To many of our customers, the face of the bank is now the ATM machine. They want to be able to get their cash out 24 hours a day or request the balance on their account or order a statement or cheque book. Last year we had over 60 million balance enquiries and nearly 15 million statements and cheque books ordered from the ATMs. Some people would say that the human element of banking is being lost, but we're providing what the customers want – when they want it.

Our transactions tend to take place either directly with our seven million customers, through our staff in the branch network where they have access to over 40,000 on-line terminals, with our sales force out in the field, who are using the latest lap-top technology or with one of the many other organizations with which we deal, such as BACS, the UK's automated clearing house, or SWIFT, the international payments' system.

To give you some idea of the money changing hands, we can transfer up to £55 billion on a peak processing day, via CHAPS, the Clearing House Automated Payments System in London. Centrally, to support these large transaction processing systems, we have some 2000 MIPS of processing power and umpteen gigabytes of storage in our data centres.

Information is extremely valuable in the banking business and much of this is obtained from our transaction processing systems. We've recently created a massive on-line relational database of customer information which ranks among the largest in the world.

continues

---

continued

For the first time, we've seen a levelling off of the volume of paper in the banking system. There's no doubt in my mind that we shall see a reduction in paper transactions in the years ahead as we move towards on-line and real-time transaction processing. This gives us the opportunity of making better use of the information we can obtain from these transactions, as we redesign our business processes to provide better customer service, to become more competitive and even perhaps to use our strength to enter new markets.

The newer technologies such as image processing and client server architectures will play an important part in this respect. On-line and real-time processing of credit card and debit card transactions will also help us better manage our personal customer base and will help us fight the fraudsters. The number of card transactions currently referred for authorization is still quite low – only about 15% in the UK whereas in the USA it's nearly 85%. While I doubt we'll get to that level, we expect we'll get up to between 50–60% in the not-too-distant future. Smart card technology could also play a part in helping to cut the level of plastic card misuse and fraud. But in the short term we favour the use of Personal Identification Numbers (PINS) at the point-of-sale. Increasingly, the information we can obtain from transactions regarding buying and usage patterns is of value. Because the more we're able to analyse our database, the more accurately we can target and market to our customers. It will also lead to increased efficiencies within the bank and give us more reliable data with which to run our business.

As Professor Michael Earl (1992) has said 'It is the information content of a transaction that is the most valuable resource.' On-line computer systems are now the lifeblood of many varied and diverse businesses and not just the domain of banks and other financial institutions. No manager or executive can afford to ignore this. Executives need to review their strategies as we move further into the information age.

Why involvement is important

Building IT for competitive advantage requires a dialogue between the people who know the business and the people who understand the capabilities of the information technology. By means of this dialogue, managers can create a shared sense of how the technology should work and what it should do.

Different approaches to involvement include top-down, bottom-up and middle-out. In top-down development, a set of specifications is laid out by top management. They then pass the specifications to people to implement the system. There is little dialogue between the people who conceive the idea of the system and those who have to build it.

In bottom-up development, people performing operational activities find a new way of working that improves on a standard operating procedure. They write the system and the benefits 'bubble-up' to the organization. This development method occurs outside the normative domains of the organization. In other words, it is a fluke.

Middle-out development requires a dialogue. In this method of development, managers interpret the strategic directions and measure the resources of the firm. They make decisions and judgements about how the strategic hopes and operational capabilities of the firm can interact on a pragmatic basis. Business managers and technology managers work as a team to pull systems together.

Involvement on a hands-on basis allows new technologies to be crafted into the organization. Innovation can be achieved through strapping new technologies to new business capabilities. Involvement allows flexibility in the organization to understand the connection between short-term needs and long-term strategic directions.

Part of the involvement of top management is to give the CIO a mandate to create organizational change. Dr Diane Wilson, a researcher at the Massachusetts Institute of Technology, describes the mandate a CIO should be given to bring about organizational change:

> The CIO must have a mission sanctioned by top management and that is believed in by line management. This statement should state clearly that the IT organization is an agent of business change. This means that they have the *ability* to facilitate changes in work processes, job definitions and roles, reward systems and even product, market or business strategies if there is an opportunity to apply IT in a strategic way. *Ability* means experience and knowhow with methodologies, tools and concepts needed to analyse existing work and information flows and to design and implement new business processes.

Involvement then is, quite simply, the organizational commitment to change with the use of IT at every level of the organization.

The 'hybrid' manager

Managers who have an ability to understand both the business direction and the technological capability are of high value. Peter Keen coined the phrase 'hybrid' manager to mean someone who attempts to blend the two skills.

Professor Michael Earl at the London Business School and Dr David Skyrme of Templeton College, Oxford, further defined the hybrid manager as:

> people with strong technical skills and adequate business knowledge, or vice versa ... hybrids are people with technical skills able to work in user areas doing a line or functional job, but adept at developing and implementing IT application ideas.

Earl and Skyrme gave several reasons why organizations need hybrid managers:

(1) IT applications that have strategic advantage tend to come from the line
(2) alignment of business processes and technical capability requires an understanding of many facets of the business by teams who are able to collaborate on business problems where IT capabilities can potentially play a role
(3) the strategic focus of information systems evolves over time, as do the relationships between business and IT managers.

Building successful partnerships between information systems workers and business workers is essential for the development of strategic information capabilities. The importance of developing hybrids is often understated in companies, yet no skill could be more necessary in enabling companies to leverage the strategic power of business processes and systems.

Training

IT training is an on-going activity because using IT is not only a skill learned by conceptual study, but it is also a skill that must be practised to be used effectively. Building the skills of the business manager involves learning about information flows and technologies and how these relate to the business.

Evidence from a number of studies (1992) suggests that most managers do not receive more than a week's IT training a year. Those who do are often not given access to technology with which to experiment on the job. When IT is introduced as an integral part of work, however, learning accelerates. Bond traders in the securities markets seemed to learn overnight how to operate complex screens and ordering programs. In fact, it was the organizations' commitment to placing orders and running an electronic market that made the difference. Today, we can see many industries moving to the electronic marketplace.

Using consultants

One way to integrate IT into the business quickly is to bring in outside professionals to design ways to use IT in the workplace. They can be responsible for designing and implementing programs to identify the strategic directions of the company, designing IT platforms to support the business and organizing a plan for change throughout the company.

Consultants can be managed by paying attention to the terms of the contract laid down between the company and the consulting firm. Since much of the desired result is intangible and hard to measure, specifications of consulting contracts are difficult to write and enforce. The direction of the project may also change within the assignment. A sound basis for any project is to have a good relationship between the company and the consultants. The best measure of a strong alliance between company and consulting firm is in the quality of the relationship between the two parties.

Executive information systems

One way top management is often brought into the habit of using IT is through executive information systems. These systems bring together the company's key performance measures into a database that is accurate, up-to-date, easy to use and accessible to its top executives.

The use of executive information systems has been so successful that many firms are now developing key indicator strategic systems (KISS) to allow more executives and managers to access this key information. As these systems grow, more and more middle managers can have access to the systems. Access can also develop on a global basis.

As EIS turn to KISS, the systems often gain more capabilities: more topics are covered by the systems; the query facility includes more flexibility in terms of manipulating the data and generating reports, and graphics and communications capabilities are extended and become more sophisticated.

Management View 10
John Watson, Director of Human Resources and Information Management, British Airways

At British Airways, John Watson, Director of Human Resources and Information Management believes that the airline's customer database is one of the most valuable assets management can use. He says:

> British Airways is becoming global. We have always been an international airline. It is essential for BA to have an information flow everywhere we operate.
>
> We create our competitive advantage by customer service, product differentiation and keeping our cost structure flexible. All this requires excellent information management.
>
> The analysis of data on customer preferences is fundamental to our decision-making process. Our customer database is becoming more important. The more intelligence we can get out of the

continues

---

continued

         customer database, the more we can feed the selling machine of British Airways.

         Building a customer database is a sophisticated art. It is important to collect data at every point the customer contacts.

         British Airways' strategy over the next few years is to grow by acquisition to be the leading global airline. Currently, the airline is the world's largest international passenger airline and the eighth largest in the world overall. BA has a flight taking off every two minutes, with 261,000 flights in 1992 carrying a total of 25 million passengers and 500,000 tonnes of cargo. Their differentiating factor in all this is their customer service: they adapt to customer needs and wants more quickly and perhaps more gracefully than any other airline.

Action checklist

  (1) Who has access to IT in your company? Do business people as well as IT people have access to IT in your company?

  (2) Are business managers involved in systems design and implementation, and if so in what roles?

  (3) Are you a 'hybrid' manager? Are there many in your firm?

  (4) Does your company offer IT training to business managers and business training to IT managers?

  (5) Does your company have an executive information system in place?

References

Foreword by Michael E. in Daniels, N. C. (1992). *On-line transaction processing: enhancing your business strategy.* The Economist Intelligence Unit, Special Report No. P666. London, October

London Business School (1992). Hybrid managers: what do we know about them? London Business School Working Paper No. 5, London

10

Major trends in the management of business IT

- As IT systems deal with information, efficient IT systems can help with control and coordination throughout an organization.
- Measuring IT effectiveness is a good way of measuring responsiveness to markets.
- Mainframes are becoming central data manipulators, or connectors for PCs. Open systems architecture will ultimately connect all systems seamlessly, but there are significant turf disputes between vendors to resolve first, as it removes the client's dependency on systems.
- Vast improvements are being made in technical communications development; many combinations of visual and audio techniques are already available. This will cut down the need for some face-to-face meetings.
- Companies should invest in a portfolio of IT systems to suit different purposes.
- Databases and sophisticated IS are vital to enable staff to answer complex customer enquiries in real-time.
- Many systems now in development, such as imaging, obviate the need for paper-based transactions.
- IT can help the optimal design of work time and roles for people in organizations.
- Work on computer languages may mean even faster information processing and as yet undreamed of business applications of IT.
- The cost of IT development has led to the formation of consortia between companies with common problems.

- Computer security does not receive proper attention.
- Knowledge of IT is a vital requirement for all business managers in the 1990s.

The management of business IT changes over time. This chapter considers the 10 major trends for the 1990s:

(1)   Improving management coordination and control over the business
(2)   Integrating the centralizing and decentralizing forces of the business
(3)   Making use of connectivity and currency to build a reliable network
(4)   Managing IT portfolios
(5)   Supporting the knowledge worker
(6)   Expanding the use of a range of multimedia
(7)   Changing work design and roles
(8)   Generating systems with business application development tools
(9)   Building interorganizational systems
(10) Ensuring effective emergency back-up.

Improving management coordination and control

Because IT systems deal with information, and handling information efficiently is the root of coordinating and controlling a business, the progressive implementation of IT will lead to measurable improvements in coordination and control of the whole organization. However, IT systems must be constructed in such a way that managers can readily understand how to apply them to business objectives. Harvard's Professor James Cash described the problem: 'The trouble is that in most companies management control systems and organizational design using IT's capabilities are treated as separate disciplines.'

How can the efficiency of a system be measured? What unit of analysis should be considered? How does IT facilitate a firm's adjustment to market change? Developing an effectiveness index which measures how effective IT is in integrating with the management's business objectives is, in fact, measuring the firm's market responsiveness, as well as its control and coordination.

David Norton, president of Nolan, Norton & Co., gave an industry example:

If you can measure it, you can manage it. Identifying the key measures of performance involves defining the strategic linkage between the investment in IT and what you are trying to do in the marketplace.

During the late 1970s Credco, a credit card division of a services organization, was a major factor in the marketplace, marketing through regional sales and service centres. It was undergoing rapid growth as the emerging industry attempted to define new customers for its credit services. Credco considered its comparative advantage to be its ability to manage risk. It would extend credit to groups that competitors would avoid, knowing that the company's superior practices of risk management would allow it to make a profit. As volumes grew, however, significant stresses were put on the ability of branch offices to manage risk.

In 1977 a decision was made to install the Branch Management System (BMS), a decision support system designed to improve account management. Prior to BMS, Credco was spending an average of $1100 per employee on IT. The average branch employee was capable of managing 600 accounts per year. In 1983, after the Branch Management System had been installed, the average IS investment per employee had increased from $1100 to $5000. The productivity of an average branch employee increased from 600 to 1000 accounts per year. The productivity gains meant that Credco was able to support the dramatic growth it experienced in business volumes between 1976 and 1983 with virtually no increase in branch staff. The staff stability contributed to a higher risk management process.

Credco increased its annual IS investment by $3900 per employee. As a result of investments, it received annual cost savings in excess of $100 m, or an equivalent of $18,000 per employee – an annual ROI of approximately five times (Norton, 1988).

The IT performance measure – number of accounts handled per employee – is also a measure of improved control over costs and profits.

Many executives are creating their own systems to track key performance measures in their companies. These executive information systems (EIS) are specially developed software programs that lock in user-defined key business indicators, such as the number of new products developed over time; numbers and classifications of customer transactions; and key economic indicators. The systems are developed to give top management a bird's eye view of the key trends in the business. EIS help management to control and coordinate the business, and are the fastest growing sector of the business software market.

Integration: centralization/decentralization

With the proliferation of technologies, a major issue is centralization/ decentralization and the need for integration. As Dr John Spackman, director of computing and information at British Telecom, said: 'The trick is to provide an integrated corporate information network in a constantly changing environment, which can combine information from various sources and is responsive to managers' requests' (1990).

In the heyday of the mainframe, centralization of IT resources was the only IT management method open. Large, central machines processed data along with programmed instructions describing what to do with the data. 'Dumb' terminals (terminals without processing power) communicated with the mainframe either in a real-time (as we speak) mode, or within a few seconds, or in 'batch' mode, through overnight or delayed processing. Centralization of all processing and data management activities meant that business users dealt with applications remotely: that is, they almost always had to go through the data processing department to describe their information needs.

With the advent of the microprocessor ...

In the 1980s microprocessors, chips that provided the 'dumb' terminals with processing and data management facilities, entered the computing scene. Decentralization of computing power became possible, which meant computing power could be in the hands of the users. In 1989 IBM created more revenue from the sales of microbased technology than from sales of mainframes.

Wider use of PCs created a new problem. Business users would often go out and buy various software and hardware to meet their needs without consulting the overall computer strategy as a whole. This created 'islands of technology', in other words several different types of computing power that did not communicate. Connecting the micro power to mainframe capability would mean a change in role for the mainframe.

In moving away from the mainframe, microbased workstations that were more powerful than PCs were developed with higher quality graphics, fast processing speed and power and more memory capacity. Initially designed for the scientific community but quickly taken up by the financial community, workstations initiated the move of power to the users. The use of workstations in business has expanded where significant local processing is needed, such as in manufacturing computer-aided design (CAD) and computer-aided machinery (CAM) and in financial securities dealing and marketing operations. Workstations are capable of communicating in seconds around the world and have highly designed layouts that enable business people to use the processing easily.

... the role of the mainframe is changing

As applications are moved from the central mainframes to the microbased platforms, companies are beginning to use their mainframes as large data manipulators, or as connectors for the various microbased platforms. An important role for the mainframe is to act as a client-server, a machine capable of picking up complex messages from one machine and routing them to others. This is a valuable function as networks develop. Rather than being the central controller, then, the new role for the mainframe is to form part of the core coordination of computer power. The mainframe market is still growing, at perhaps 10% worldwide, not quite the rate of the micro market, at 15–20% for PCs and 20–30% for workstations. Supercomputers – a grade of elegance above the mainframe, at the top of the range in speed, processing capability and image manipulation – are a specific requirement to meet the needs of such organizations as NASA.

Integrating the technologies

With distributed computing putting power into the hands of the business users, the elusive goal is to provide seamless, transparent integration among technologies. The power in the systems is the synergy they provide to the business, information being the lifeblood that holds the business together.

A major effort in the direction of integration has been the attempt to build a capability for open systems architecture. This would ultimately mean that all the various technologies would be able to connect to each other. The onus to integrate the technologies would be on the vendors rather than on the businesses that purchase the technology. This is the end of a very long exercise of oligopolistic power that the vendors have practised both because of their different approaches to technology and, to some extent, their desire to tie their customers in to their own particular systems. In the past, buying one vendor's machinery meant that to be able to build on to that platform in a compatible way, the company would have to keep buying from the same vendor.

In the integrated workplace, where mainframes are used as connectors rather than controllers, the technology challenge shifts to being able to handle multiple technologies. This could mean that businesses will be able to select the best technologies for various applications. However, open systems architecture is in the early stages and is developing: it is not here yet. Nevertheless it is important for businesses to support vendor efforts to move in the open systems direction, for it means a move towards greater integration of information power for the companies.

Connectivity and currency

Telecomms is fundamentally a value-added technology with phenomenal technical complexity. The business manager wants to know what IT can do, that is whatever services can be made available on his or her desk rather than how the IT is done. In some senses, the tragedy is that it does almost always work: we have 99% reliability in the case of voice, so the complexity is transparent to the users. When something goes wrong, business people are not prepared. Business managers want reliability, but they also need to be aware that the interactions require in-depth IT.

In our business telecomms have had a dramatic effect. The single European market exists because of telecomms. Today it is necessary to recognize the linkage of business strategy and IT. It is necessary to understand simultaneously what the capabilities of the technology are and how that can effect how business is carried out. Some companies develop a business plan, and then modify IT to fit the plan in a sequential process which leads to the danger of computerizing the manual processes. Managers must integrate efforts so that the business and IT capabilities can be properly integrated. Of course it is hard to translate the basic benefits of communications to the balance sheet, but that is the fundamental utility of the business. We couldn't operate our business without great communications.

This comment from Simon Allen, voice manager at Bankers' Trust, reflected the necessity for great communications. Integration requires connectivity. As the market for systems integration grows, from $3.5 bn in 1987 to a projected $12 bn in 1992, communications will provide the backbone.

Connecting information networks for companies ...

Making use of the power to connect information networks to provide current information where it is needed is helping many companies compete on a time basis. Reuters, providers of market information to stock exchanges, is experiencing a boom in business as the need for up-to-date international market information soars.

Fax and satellite-based communications combine to provide a powerful network for transmitting information around the world. The *Financial Times* prints regional copies simultaneously in the UK, Germany, France, the USA and Japan using this combination. Satellites are expensive and there is a limit to how many can be sent up. Fibre optics and radio waves are offering two alternative communications backbones.

Radio frequency is a less expensive alternative for connecting the workplace, particularly if the workplace is outside an office. Radio-based data transmissions have the advantage of being mobile. Field data can be entered directly into the computer system without requiring complex technologies. These systems are particularly useful in delivery-oriented parts of the business or in businesses in which the customer is visited on location.

... and individuals

Other types of networked applications are also growing rapidly. Communications for the individual are becoming more commonly available: electronic mail, faxes and voice mail. Electronic mail networks allow business managers to communicate on a formal or informal basis. Faxes have become the accepted way to transmit business documents in just a decade, with over seven million fax stations existing worldwide. Advances in the technology continue, with a convergence towards voice.

Within a decade it may be commonplace to send a memo over a work-station which includes a fax of documents, including graphics, along with a voice message. Communications will further progress towards the open environment by offering individuals an assortment of technologies to use and combine. In February 1990 Steve Jobs demonstrated the NeXT machine which is capable of providing powerful combinations of communications capability. Enumerating the business benefits, Mr Jobs said: 'The new applications will help cut meeting time and increase an individual's power to communicate.' Meetings will no longer require the physical presence of the participants. While the benefits of face-to-face meetings are highly valued, at times managers will choose to communicate through conference networks via IT systems.

Mobile communications have grown dramatically. These are based on cellular technology and again costs are coming down. In Scandinavia one in 20 individuals owns a mobile phone. In the future mobile phones will certainly become the norm, enabling fixed point communication from wherever an individual happens to be. In a further advance, the technologies will converge once again to combine data access with voice recognition. The thrust of the trend is towards currency of data and immediate communications.

Management View 11

Professor Peter Keen   Telecommunications, Time and the Business Manager

Telecommunications is what I call 'the invisible factor.' What we've actually got with telecommunications is a business resource which is here already yet we have a management culture which doesn't know anything about it.

If you take any industry where electronic delivery, for example electronic telecommunications, could change the competitive rules, in every

continues

continued

single one of those industries 60% of the firms have gone out of business within the last ten years. More importantly, at least two of the firms that have disappeared were in the top ten. If you were betting on airlines in 1978, you would have put Pan Am and Eastern right at the top because of the route structure. If you were betting on retailers, you would have picked Sears. If you were betting on banking, you would have picked Bank of America.

It's very hard for firms to challenge their basic assumptions. Telecommunications is a great subversive factor for organizations because it is not part of what I call your knowledge anchors, those things that you treat as part of your basic management assumptions.

How do you get into a position where you take something like electricity for granted? Maxwell invented electricity, but in a sense, it was always there. Maxwell invented electricity through his equations and this was the first time it passed into the language. So, he created the linguistic distinction called electricity, which meant people can now manage electricity or think about it or plan it.

At a certain point, technology when it becomes such an integral part of our day-to-day function, it is like breathing air, it gets taken for granted. We are not yet at the stage where we take computers for granted. 'User friendly' just means 'less user hostile'. We are not yet at the stage where we take telecommunications for granted, but we are beginning to do so with, for example, cable TV.

Information is not a thing, it is not a commodity, it is a relationship. Information is understanding.

Managers say they're uncomfortable about telecommunications because they're aware of the fact that they don't quite know what it is. Most people do not realize that ATMs use telecommunications. We are all changing our behaviour and ordering from electronic mail order catalogue companies: that's telecommunications. We are beginning to use electronic filing with the tax services. We're in the self-conscious stage with telecommunications.

Executives and managers should be asking themselves first: where is the point of event that triggers a sale? Then put telecommunications behind that point of event. Second, how should your flow of logistics work from that point of event if you didn't have time and locational constraints? Finally, managers should scan the competitive environment and ask: is there any sign that someone is doing it?

Remember, if somebody does it, 50% of the firms will leave the industry. What is the mechanism for this? We call it telecommunications.

Videoconferencing is a management tool that helps to build strategic intent. CEOs are able to communicate by 'walking about electronically'. The reality of the commitment of business leaders is demonstrated by the use of videoconferencing.

How do you mobilize a culture where the culture no longer comes to work? How do you mobilize a culture that is global? If you are Unilever Netherlands, what have you got in common with Unilever Korea? If you are

continues

continued

somebody in Citibank, you are in the information business in a number of different areas, so what does it mean to be a Citibanker? There has to be some welding of the strategic intent issue, the values, and the belief in the values of the leader. Telecommunications is the media for the message.

In the old era of IT, the question to business managers would be: what application do you choose? We are now in the integration era in which managers focus on: how do you get out of organizational functional compartments and strengthen products? When managers succeed in this new environment, you can't tell the difference between the culture, the technology and the process.

If you talk about aligning telecommunications strategy with the business strategy, it's too late. If you need to align them, then you've already lost. The big problem is language. What we've got is a lot of specialists who create a language for IT that says 'This is different!' It also says 'We will do it for you, not with you.'. It says methodology means 'I've got a secret.'

The real issue for executives, forget about telecommunications, forget about information, just think about what is the best logistical flow that is possible in the industry and who's doing it. What you will always find is that someone has changed the rules of the game through communications and when that happens.

If you start tracking the point of event from the customer's viewpoint, your logistics will change. What you find is that if you look at that chain as separate divisions or functions, you are right up against the re-engineering problem: how can we reduce the number of steps it takes to accomplish something, or reduce time in our business processes. When you start putting into combination business thinking and communications, you change the competitive dynamics. You can't think about re-engineering without telecommunications, you just can't do it.

If you look at the 're' phenomenon, there are all these 're' words around: restructuring, realigning, re-engineering and there will soon be a 're-re' industry. The word does not appear in business books before 1989. In Tom Peters' earlier books, the only 're' word is revolution, now 're' actually means 'try again'. What I think is happening is that we have a paucity of imagination around the fact that something is happening, we don't know what the hell it is, so we say 're', for example, redesign.

The reason this is happening in the basic vocabulary of business language is that businesses are now being defined by customer driven points of event and the barriers of time and location are being removed. Until recently, every single aspect of organizational design was built around time and location. That is why we have paper, to deal with the time delay of communication. It's the reason we have functional departments.

The 're' word is a signal that something is going on and we don't quite know what it is. By the time we do find out what the paradigm for the future is, it will already have happened.

Telecommunications changes the basics of business in ways that we may not be able to predict.

Information networks are growing

Information networks within companies are on the increase. Local area networks (LAN) are growing at 15% worldwide. Networking across organizations to enable data access and real-time team work is growing. Groupware is a new area of software development which allows several members of a team to work together simultaneously on a single project.

Information from outside the firm will become increasingly important as world competition increases. Demand for access to databanks and electronic libraries which provide market information will rise. IBM estimates that '50% of the electronic information consumed in the UK is supplied offshore from the USA. Basically information networks have the facility to supply information products and services from anywhere in the globe into any free market' (Worlock, 1990). This is another addition to the communications infrastructure.

IT portfolios

IT is not a one-flavour activity. Different business purposes require different systems approaches. For example, applications built for specific business activities are called retail systems. An example would be the uses to which the application of automatic identification has been put. Bar-coding, magnetic stripe, radio-frequency tagging, optical reader recognition (OCR) and smart cards are all examples of automatic identification technologies. Their purpose is to label and identify each product so that the recognition is made in machine-readable form. When a product passes by a grocery till and is pushed through a scanner, the store forms a record of the status of the inventory of the product.

Utility systems provide the core of the company's capability, such as communications or data management. Examples of utility applications would be accounts and subscriptions. Venture applications experiment with new systems. Having a computer lab to test new technologies increases knowledge of how to manage the technology and decreases project risks.

Not all IT has to be developed in-house. Companies may decide that packages are more appropriate depending on how close they are to their business needs. If a software house can provide the same functionality, this may be a route to consider. Many companies fall into the trap of reorganizing their business processes to fit the software rather than the other way round. In terms of investment this may make sense. Or a vendor may run the computer system, managing the computer facilities for a business.

The essence of having a thriving applications portfolio is to balance the demand from business users for IT with the supply and the company's ability to manage IT. Managing different types of demand portfolios (retail, utility and venture) along with different sources of IT supply (in-house and out-sourced) is the challenge of planning and implementing the portfolio.

Supporting the knowledge worker

As workers handle increased complexity and as markets become more service-oriented, knowledge workers rely more on IT to complement their knowledge of the business. For example, if someone calls up an airline to reserve a seat, a credit card company to check their balance, or even a retail company to check if a product is in stock and how the product performs, they are relying on that person's knowledge of the product. Some of this knowledge is so extensive, as in the case of airline schedules (subject to change) and the balance with the credit card company, or may require such in-depth knowledge of product performance characteristics, that the number of variables are impossible to keep either in a human mind or in a split second reference system without the aid of computers.

Databases developed for knowledge workers provide an extension to the knowledge of the person performing the work. Systems may also be equipped with decision logic to play scenarios of options for decisions the person can take. Expert systems offer a higher level of knowledge than the person may have, and help to reduce the number of people that have to deal with a request.

Knowledge systems play a big role in training. In product training, for example, people learn selling skills. They can learn about products, then test themselves for technique on interactive video. Alternatively they can learn about live situations that are difficult to duplicate, and so they are simulated. Jeff Cameron, at the frontier of interactive video management training in the USA at American Safety Video Publishers in Naples, Florida, designs systems for emergency rescue squads. He said:

> With interactive video, the learning rate is much higher, people can perceive more about experience with multidimensional communications. Sound, colour and excellent graphics create a realistic crisis that the rescue teams have to deal with. Periodic quizzing and intelligent branching, to throw in unexpected circumstances, test the team's ability to deal with simulations of real-world environments.

Multimedia

Business usage of multimedia is expanding, with images replacing words as communication media. As the number of products and markets to monitor increases for financial dealers, the number of messages they receive becomes complex. Images and symbols decrease the complexity of data by summarizing the information in pictorial form. 'Windows' of images are suppressed or brought forward as and when they are needed. Various estimates put worldwide sales of multimedia at $20 bn in 1993. Companies are finding more uses for multimedia as costs decrease.

Companies are moving from paper-based to electronic-based information. Thornton May, director of imaging research at the Nolan Norton Institute, said: 'Customers and markets wait for no man – and particularly not a man searching for paper-based files.' The largest current users of imaging are governments, financial services, insurance and credit card companies. Companies are moving towards the paperless society because paper-based communications slow business processes. By replacing the paper-based receipt of transaction with images, companies save time, money and space by transmitting information electronically. With imaging systems everyone with access to the system can have immediate up-to-date information about work in progress.

The major barrier to imaging and the use of multimedia rests with the management of business processes. Some workers are reluctant to change to the new media. With training, and a comprehensive communication plan about how media can redesign business processes, the greatest successes are achieved.

Other forms of media that are increasingly used are microfiche and microfilm, optical disk (a fast, durable, storage media which has a higher degree of disaster resistance and increased space) and voice response/record systems.

Work design and roles

Business success in the future will apply to companies with business managers who understand and grasp the opportunities of managing information in new ways, and with IT managers who understand the business. As previously mentioned, much discussion today is about the 'hybrid' manager: the manager who understands about both managing the business and managing IT. Management's recognition of the business/technology linkage is contributing to the changing role of corporate management.

Vic Mutnick, corporate vice-president of New York Life Insurance Company, discussed the learning process that managers go through:

They want to know more as they get involved. We just taught sales managers how to use New York Life Sales System, our leading-edge field agent system. This allows agents to enter data from the field, query customer and product databases, analyse customer needs and recommend the most suitable New York Life product. At first they were looking for the 'on' button. Within an hour they were asking how much central office information they could get at; then they realized they could answer most of the underwriting questions in the field, which meant they could confirm applications in minutes. That's the part of implementation they want to know: what will it do for my business, then how do I work it, that's all. They don't care about the boxes.

Case 10.1   New York Life Insurance Company – New York Life Integrated Selling System

Context

New York Life Insurance (NYL) is one of the USA's largest insurance companies, with income in 1989 of $15.3 bn, total assets of $46.6 bn and life insurance in force of $300.8 bn. NYL offers products such as universal life, mutual funds, partnership investments, guaranteed investment contracts and securities products. NYL is unique in that the company relies on agents as the sole sales channel for its insurance products.

Why change?

The insurance industry is becoming more competitive as the speed with which information can be processed increases. Time to process claims and answer queries, time to close sales for agents and time to create new financial products to suit the markets, are all considerations for increasing competitive edge. The management of NYL, in supporting the field agents, decided to create a channel for information that would enable the agents to tap in directly to the customer and product information the company holds.

Vision

The Mission Statement of NYL is reproduced in Chapter 5.

What NYL did

NYL built the New York Life Sales System. The system offers information relating to the full range of selling activities: prospecting, needs analysis,

continues

continued

illustrations of concepts, underwriting, processing and commissions planning. This is all available on a portable computer that travels where the agent travels. It is a system that brings together the basic resources that agents need and use in their business. It was specifically designed to be flexible enough for agents to use as much or as little as they see fit. 'Being able to generate several different illustrations right at the point-of-sale is one of the most amazing aspects of the portable computer,' says Richard Paules.

Most of the parts of the system existed already. This effort concentrated on integration. NYL Sales System 'incorporates what we've had in the past, and builds upon that for what we can and will do in the future,' says Lester Schoenberg, senior vice-president.

Outcome

Agents have taken to the system. In addition to helping the agent demonstrate products and print contracts, and hence close sales more effectively, NYL Sales System reduces the back-room costs of both the agent and NYL. The drop in costs is due to the elimination of loops of enquiry between the agent and NYL. Now the agent has direct access to information to resolve operating questions.

Future

NYL has proved that the whole system is greater than the sum of its parts. The company is further integrating information systems to provide greater efficiencies and scope for agents and NYL employees. Richard Wecker, senior vice-president of agency, states: 'NYL Sales System is an investment in our agents and in the agency system, and demonstrates our commitment to the field force. New York Life is on the fast track to the future.'

As more people gain skills with technology, telecommuting – or working from a remote site of the user's choice, sometimes at home, sometimes on a business trip – is becoming more common. Some businesses are exploring the possibilities of flexible working hours, allowing people to decide which hours they will work at home and requiring a lesser involvement in the office. The businesses save on overheads, and staff can adjust their own schedules to suit their lifestyles. Professor Lotte Bailyn of the Massachusetts Institute of Technology has researched telecommuting. 'Some people don't work at their best during the day between the hours of 9 a.m. to 5 p.m. Studies indicate that people have varying productivity patterns. When allowed to determine how they will allocate their time to work, productivity almost always increases.'

The available workforce is growing as the demand for people with IT skills increases, but not nearly fast enough. Ten to twenty per cent of jobs in

IT-related areas go unfilled in many developed countries, and in developing countries the search is on for qualified people to bring up the standard of knowledge.

IT starts, carries on, ends and begins again with people. As projects involve more people, teamwork will become essential. The attitude of employees skilled in IT is important. The requirements in the future to develop human resources will increase. As Dr Alan Cane, head of the IT desk at the *Financial Times*, observed (1990):

> There will be wide-ranging changes in recruitment and training, and improved career prospects for DP staff. The aim must be to create an environment where staff feel motivated and productive and know that their individual efforts will be appreciated and acknowledged: without these investments it will not be possible to staff the systems function so that it can satisfy the new and changing demands being made by the business.

Developments in computer languages

'Higher level languages' are languages the computer can understand which are coming closer to human language. In the beginning computers only understood combinations of '1' (the switch is on) and '0' (the switch is off). By various combinations of 1s and 0s, a human alphabet could be supported. The machine languages remained the foundation so that the machine could process the data quickly. Computer languages are becoming more like human language. Very soon computers will be able to understand human language. For the business manager this means that user languages are easier to understand, such as the latest database packages and packaged software like Lotus.

Another productivity improvement has been the use of fourth generation application generators (referring to the fact that the language is a fourth quantum leap in the history of IT programming developments). CASE, computer-aided software engineering tools, and object-oriented languages are examples of fourth generation applications. The object of these is to increase the productivity of program generation by creating modules of code to build programs on, rather than relying on less powerful tools, and to make them easier for users to work with.

With the advent of palm-top computing and the use of light pens, very soon we shall rely on computers to interpret complex human symbols such as individual handwriting and interpret them accurately. Another development is 'groupware', software that enables several people to work on the same problem together. In the near future, individuals will be able to communicate from wherever they are via individual systems to group systems, allowing the definition of work organizations to be changed to include contemporaneous networks of people. As computer languages develop, the flexibility of work will increase as the manipulation and sharing of symbolic languages becomes easier.

Interorganizational systems

Interorganizational systems provide functionality to at least two corporate entities. Thus supplier/customer systems and systems among companies are interorganizational systems. Some examples are travel companies connecting with travel agents, insurance companies developing products with other insurance companies in strategic alliances, automobile manufacturers connecting with dealers, retailers and suppliers, and governmental organizations connecting with private business, as in the case of customs connecting with shippers to facilitate the smooth passage of goods.

The advantages of interorganizational systems are that they decrease the time it takes to communicate to parties, the cost of the systems can be shared, and business relationships are enhanced by being able to see over the wall a bit to understand operational and management issues.

As the price of developing IT continues to rise, companies are forming consortia to produce systems to increase their return on investment. Thus many of the banks that created automated teller machine (ATM) networks, as early adaptors of the technology carried the full weight of investment themselves. Banks entering the niche later on formed consortia to share the cost of development of networks that would rival the market leaders.

Emergency back-up

'Nothing can go wrong, can go wrong, can go wrong ...' What happens if things do go wrong? Fire, fraud and illegal entry can all cause significant harm to a company's information. In fact, that is just what happened to Digital Equipment, a major IT supplier, but it had its systems up and running again in a matter of hours and has used the experience to develop a security back-up service to customers.

Security has many aspects. There is the security that authorizes entry: fingerprints, signatures and retinal scanning. These biometric systems are increasingly used to test a person's identity. There is the problem of software viruses – software programs that contain elements that are harmful to other programs and create havoc such as printing 'Bilbo Lives!' on the user's screen while simultaneously erasing his or her disk. 'Hacking', the illegal entry and then directing of a part of the computer system by an unauthorized person, is perhaps the greatest threat since the method of entry is difficult to anticipate.

One of the earliest instances of computer fraud involved a man who entered the payroll system of a large utility company. The program he wrote into the system extracted a few pennies from each person's paycheque, directed the money to an aggregation point and issued a cheque to him. He was caught, but only after the program had been active for several months. Since this was one of the first instances, the company pardoned him on return of the money and actually hired him to help prevent other hackers from entering the system. Years later, with many more hackers operative, most are sent to prison.

Yet most companies pay little attention to the prospect of fraud in their systems. Indications are that over 10% spend nothing on security, while over 25% incurred losses from breaches in security.

Another aspect of security involves the operating of critical systems. These are systems that control potential life or death situations. Security is highest in these information dependent systems such as hospital systems and piloting systems. Back-up and override systems are increasingly important, as a large part of rote monitoring and prescribing is handed over to machines.

Viruses

'A computer virus is a computer program that attaches copies of itself to other programs without the knowledge of the operator. Each copy will usually contain all the capability and functionality of the original virus program.' Jim Bates of Bates & Associates. (1993) *A Director's Guide to Business Security.* Director Publishing, London.

There are many different types of viruses but the two main categories are parasitic viruses which infect files, and boot sector viruses which infect disks. Understanding how computer viruses are spread is the route by which one can guard against infection.

Most viruses are introduced into a company's system by careless and unauthorized use of disks and hardware. For example, staff should not be allowed to take home disks to work on computers at home, unless that computer is in a highly secure environment. Bates cites the example of an office worker whose son plays computer games on his father's home computer and introduces an infected game disk to the system, which then infects his father's office disk which, in turn, infects the whole office system over a period of months.

Another security breach is made by staff who bring home software from exhibitions and seminars. There are anti-virus packages available now which effectively 'search and clean' disks and files. These should be an essential part of any company's risk-management programme, as well as security measures for personnel which stop the careless use of software.

Key lessons for business managers

The improved business potential IT creates: what to do next

As companies compete more aggressively using information, knowledge of IT will affect the way management carry out their evaluation of the business as a whole and, especially, its level of IT investment.

Alvin Toffler wrote in *Power Shift* (1990) that the knowledge monopolies are losing power due to the accessibility of information brought about by the information age. For managers to be successful in the new business environment, they must learn more about ways to access and use knowledge. This is a game that business managers must be a part of or risk losing track of one of the fundamental business constructs for the 1990s.

This book emphasizes the need for management involvement in every phase of business IT. Keeping up with global trends of IT and how companies are using IT to open up new markets is an important part of the management agenda.

By thinking about IT as a set of maps stretched on the canvas of a company's operations, management can plan and build IT to develop a powerful portfolio of capabilities. By building a business vision, taking into account the roles IT can play, management will be opening up new avenues of exploration for business opportunity.

Benchmarking the company's skills and growth in experience of managing IT helps management to measure progress *vis-à-vis* competitors or potential competitors. By analysing the investment, where the investment is made and how closely the investment matches the strategic objectives of the firm, management can better manage maximum returns.

Moving towards the future, companies that invest now in building a knowledge base to manage business IT will encourage managers to seek out new ways of doing business. The challenge of IT for business managers is ultimately to become involved with one of the most powerful business forces to shape the global business world for decades to come.

Action checklist

(1) What are the top three business environment issues affecting your company's future? How does information play a role? What does this mean for your company's information technology management challenge?

(2)   How will your company leverage intellectual capital in the future? What will the supporting systems have to be capable of to support this knowledgeware?

(3)   Is your company currently undertaking a redesign of key business processes? What prompted the action? What part does information management play in the restructuring?

(4)   How information dependent is your company? Are there possibilities to build competitive advantage with information technology? How is your company going about this?

(5)   What are the three most important steps your company should be taking toward the global information age? What is your challenge as a manager in playing a key role? Can you make a difference to the direction of your company?

References

Cane, A. (1990). Staff shortages bite, *Financial Times*, 16 October

Norton, D. P. (1988). The economics of computing in the advanced stages. *Stage by Stage*. Massachusetts: Nolan, Norton & Co.

Spackman, J. (1990). The Digital Equipment Corporation Information Technology lectures at the London Business School, June

Toffler, A. (1990). *Power Shift*. Bantam Books, a division of Bantam, Doubleday, Dell Publishing Group Inc., New York

Worlock, D. (1990). council president of the European Information Industry Association, Dialling into networks. *1992 Now*, IBM Europe, France, April

11

Management concerns for the future

- As the business environment faces change, businesses are restructuring the way they use IT.
- Companies are attempting to become global from different starting points.
- Managers' need for new applications that focus on business-generating activities, such as customer service, are driving the development of many on-line systems.
- The commitment and involvement of top executives and managers continue to be the critical factor in building strategic IT.

Room for creative management

The value of business information depends directly upon the interaction of people, business issues and technology. In other words, the competitive value of information in a firm depends on how information is managed. Good management of information, in turn, depends upon the firm's ability to create business competencies, by integrating human and technological capabilities.

Executives and managers are working on developing methods to motivate business and technology managers to work together. Whatever management style people in the firm use to integrate resources, there is a further complication, a further set of obstacles every management team needs to address. That is, that the business environment, technology and organizational forms are in a state of flux. This is caused by the move towards the information age from the industrial age. This promises to be as major a change as the shift to the industrial age from the agricultural age. For most of us, it will mean major changes in the ways we work and live.

As we move away from the industrial age further into the information age, the ways executives and managers relate to the dimensions of time and space are changing. Distance can be overcome in many instances by the use of telecommunications and networks; time-critical resources can be pulled together over a fibre optic link. As managers, we need to rethink every aspect of what we are doing and how we are doing business.

The good news is that there is room for creative management. By looking to the future, rather than the *status quo* or the past for models of business management, today's managers can influence the strategic direction of their companies.

A key step for managers in influencing the directions of their companies is to understand the directions of the many changes facing us in the business, technology and organizational environments. The directions of many changes that are of paramount concern to managers are highlighted in this chapter.

Management View 12

Kit Grindley   Professor of Systems Automation at the London School of Economics and Price Waterhouse Consultant

To find out what the key concerns of IT managers are, I conduct a survey each year with 1000 IT executives in the UK and 5000 worldwide and update it on a quarterly basis. One of the fundamental questions we ask is: 'What are the major issues of concern you are facing today?' For the past 18 months, the leading concern has been 'cost containment', which must be due in part to the recessionary climate and will probably go away, since it has not been the primary concern for the past 25 years.

The second issue IT executives mention is 'integrating IT with corporate objectives': that is, getting the IT systems to be a part of the corporate plan. The third issue executives mention is the old chestnut; it has always been a concern of IT executives: 'meeting project deadlines in terms of cost and time'.

We see two sorts of major systems projects companies are laying down: (1) the creation of infrastructures to enable companies to do something new

continues

continued

in the business, and, once the infrastructure is in place, (2) user development with the use of fourth generation languages.

There is a bit of a breakthrough there. In 1980, a strong trend began of user spending outside the central IT department. With the advent of the personal computer, users could develop their own systems. User spend outside the central IT department has increased about 2% per year, moving up to about 21% of total spend in 1989, before the recession. Now we see that outside spend crawling back a bit. It is very expensive to spread computing around the company and to control the cost once it is out there.

To complicate it all, we have this 'open systems' trend at the moment that seems to mean different things to different people. 'Open systems' is related to the client-server approach. To some extent it encourages users to do their own thing – but things often don't work out as easily as expected.

Out-sourcing is predicted to double over the next four years, from 7% of IT expenditure now to 14% over the next few years. Out-sourcing could be applied to systems development or to the selection of mainframes and other equipment, hardware and processing.

If we take out-sourcing as a possible trend, one of the skills that will be needed in the core of the company will be not just project management but *contract* management. It is useful in some ways to compare IT to the construction industry. Construction is all about contract management; there are architects, inspectors, bricklayers, etc. Most of these roles are carried out on a subcontracting basis. We need those same contract management skills in IT management if we are going down the out-sourcing path. We need to think more about the way we give out contracts, manage them and ensure that they are done properly.

The construction analogy breaks down a bit because it is possible for an architect to draw plans with precision, whereas with business IT, we tend to change our minds during the life of the project. This makes it difficult to build models and to hold on to the controls.

Getting our requirements for a precise information architecture is a problem for the future. IT continues to have a falling-out over performance. The solution may be, in part, a new system development approach that is very detailed and emphasizes the development of prototypes.

There is tremendous emphasis now for management to identify the core strategy of the business. Executives are concentrating on, 'What makes our company different? Why is our product different? What are our distinguishing features?' The questions arise: what should executives out-source and what should be done in-house? What executives think of as differentiating capabilities are kept in-house, whereas they seek to out-source activities that do not generate competitive advantage. One potential danger is that companies rely on consultants to set standards for projects. Another danger is that many executives do not recognize that the design and control of information within their products and services can be a source of competitive advantage.

continues

continued

The culture gap between business and IT executives and managers continues to exist. It is partly a generational problem and there are a number of middle managers in companies that are simply waiting for the present board to retire. Many middle managers think that their main business is IT or critically interdependent with IT. There is, they think, an opportunity to excel with this perspective.

Very few executives in top management today came up through the IT route. Some companies that have produced wonders with IT have merely automated processes they already had. In these cases, there is no clear perception at the top of what to do with the increasingly available customer information. Customers can talk directly to top management now: companies don't need to rely solely on the store manager to interpret customer trends for them now. Many leading companies are missing the real benefits of IT because they don't realize they could carry out their business differently.

The engineering industry has a lot to teach us. Thanks to the Japanese, companies have been faced with fierce competition for the past 15 years. This has caused executives to rethink the way business is done. Activities have been reorganized so that the managers of projects can cut across functional boundaries. The Japanese realized that there should be no barriers between designers and people on the shop floor. Beyond cross-functional integration, executives and managers need to move the IT responsibility into those projects.

If there is a future for the IT executive, they are going to have to be on board, in the first division of board decision-making along with the marketing, production and chief executives. Having the right infrastructure with communications, a common corporate database and one or two high transaction processing jobs that drive databases and the strategy of the business is the key to a competitive future. Sixty to seventy per cent of IT infrastructure is of that type. This infrastructure is essential for the survival of the company today and for the major strategies of the future it is embarking on.

What then will be the key business management skills of the future? There has been a divorce of power and responsibility that has been detrimental to the development of business IT. In the past, when we promoted IT people, we gave them more and more power. Resentment built up within the company as this power encroached on the power of the other directors.

Executives need to bridge the gap between power and responsibility. This is really a plea to give the IT executive responsibility for business results. The IT executive should be responsible for corporate performance, not only for the production of IT systems. The IT executive should be responsible for producing the right systems for the business, the systems that bring results. If the IT executive actually had responsibility for corporate performance rather than just systems performance, members of the board would feel more compelled to involve themselves in working out what part of the business depends on IT for competitive advantage.

The changing business environment

The top five issues facing management today include: increasing competition, volatile economic markets, globalization, customer demand for quality and advances in IT. As companies face turbulent change in market forces, executives for the first time have explicitly listed advances in IT as a critical success factor for survival (Dr John Rockart, MIT).

Many companies are in the middle of redesigning their businesses from strategic, management and operational perspectives. Massive restructuring and downsizing initiatives are taking place in every industry, in every size company, at every level.

Globalization is driving much of the increasing competitive forces, since competition can now come from anywhere: as interdependency increases, changes in one part of the globe affect another. Globalization is influencing the ways in which information is managed.

A worldwide study attempted to define broadly the characteristics of a global company:

> The ideal global company is both a low-cost producer and customer driven. It balances global consistency with local diversity. It has a flexible product and service architecture that allows for a high level of customization. It has a highly coordinated value chain that utilizes multiple centres of excellence distributed throughout the world in the most appropriate locations.
>
> The global company can support both global and local customers with balanced global/local sales and support channels. It operates like a geodesic network that enables and encourages its employees to communicate point-to-point rather than through the hierarchical chain of command (Daniels and Daniels, 1993).

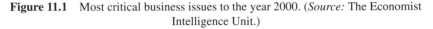

Increasing competition	47%
Volatile economic conditions	32%
Globalization	29%
Customer demand for quality	28%
Advances in information technolgy	26%

Figure 11.1 Most critical business issues to the year 2000. (*Source:* The Economist Intelligence Unit.)

The global exporter: the multinational and the multilocal

The study (Daniels and Daniels, 1993) also found that not all companies attempt to become global in the same way. In other words, companies are starting from different positions when setting out to become more global (see Figure 11.2). These models of international business are the global exporter, the multinational and the multilocal. To become a global company, managers in international companies are working at changing their current mindset, configuration of resources and management practices. The study differentiates among the models and describes some of the different ways information is managed:

> The global exporter expands into the international marketplace by pushing domestic product through an expanded, international distribution channel. Characteristics of the exporting company include a product-push view of foreign markets; maintenance of most if not all value-chain activities, except sales and service, in the home country, run by home-country nationals; and complete home-country control in management. As Figure 11.2 suggests, the exporter gets its advantage by being a low-cost producer, and has great difficulty being highly responsive to the customer.

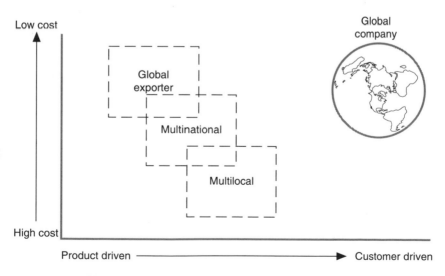

Figure 11.2   Positioning a company in a global context.

The multinational develops relatively homogeneous products or services for the world. Manufacturing is distributed around the world to exploit economies of scale and vault barriers to entry. The multinational tries to maximize the use of resources through strong central coordination, rather than flexibly integrating resources to distributed competence centres. By physically moving closer to its customers and taking advantage of scale economies, the multinational is able to deliver fairly low-cost products to most customers.

In a multinational company, headquarters plays a strong role in setting strategies, policies and establishing standards. While a matrix management structure may be in place to handle the complexity of product/service offerings in individual locations, major decisions are made by headquarters and communicated via outbound directives. Sales and delivery channels tend to be regionally controlled, with some level of autonomy from corporate headquarters, provided fairly rigid revenue and profit guidelines are met. This concern creates a bias toward the further development of home-country and major markets, since markets are often judged by profit-generating measures.

The multinational, then, still offers a primarily product-push set of strategies, while capturing economies of scale. By locating some operations in countries for cost or entry reasons, the company gathers some intelligence about local customers, and is more open to innovation than global exporters.

Customers increasingly want customization of some aspects of products and services. The multilocal specializes in local customization to meet local customer requirements. It is through customization that companies add value to commodity goods. Local sales and delivery offer customized products.

The multilocal is customer focused, responsive and flexible to local requirements. The balance of power is with the national organization. These strong national organizations operate as a set of independently operating, self-reliant and geographically dispersed units. While fostering independence and initiative, the sharing of management knowledge across boundaries is minimal, and such an approach forces unit managers to climb steep learning curves as they continuously reinvent knowledge on how to carry out the business. The multilocal company tends to duplicate a large portion of the value chain in each country where it does business, and sacrifices economies of scale in an attempt to meet local market requirements.

Multilocals do not approach the world as one business system, but rather as a set of individual markets, each to be approached separately. Because this leads to many separate and distinct sets of operating procedures, the multilocal has more difficulty than the multinational in supporting anyplace business, although it has an edge on global exporters because of the broader geographic scope. It also means that multilocals are much more mechanistic than either global exporters or multinationals.

Multilocals have to contend with high walls built around each country, as well as the strongest case of the not-invented-here syndrome. On the other hand, multilocals have a strong advantage over the other current forms in terms of cultural fit, often leading to high-value differentiated services.

We might say that a quick way to understand a global company would be to think of a company that combines the holistic approach and ability to take advantage of economies of scale of a global exporter, the strong business concept and decentralization of knowledge and decision-making found in the multinational, and the rigorous attention to cultural fit of the multilocal.

By and large, the global exporter model is one we typically see in Japanese companies; the multinational organization is an American phenomenon; and the multilocal format is one favoured by Western European companies.

An important distinction between *global* systems and *international* business systems is that in global systems, the global and local balance of information requirements for the business are taken into account at the time of the *design* of the systems, rather than adding additional capability on a country by country basis.

As customers focus on quality, customer databases that hold information about changing customer preferences are of increasing importance. Market conditions throughout the world are being more closely monitored so that changes can be understood by designers and marketers as well as manufacturers.

The systems that allow companies to work as partners to create products to serve customers are reaching across corporate borders. Many companies include plans to connect banks, suppliers, customers, shippers/transporters, brokers/dealers, customs officials and government agencies to the companies' systems to expedite the creating and handling of products and services. Finance systems capable of handling multicurrency calculations and investments, such as foreign exchange transactions, options and futures, interest rate swaps, equities and debt instruments are designed to be fast and flexible to react to the world's changing market conditions. High areas for growth for non-financial activities include databases, inventory control, booking orders, marketing and sales, warehouse management, training, education and manufacturing.

Executives and managers are aware that IT advances are important to the firm. Still, many business managers struggle with IT concepts, while older executives lack familiarity with IT capabilities. Professor Kit Grindley, a well-known authority on management concerns offers his opinions in Management View 12.

Changing technology

Awareness of the importance of business information technology is growing as Figure 11.3 shows. Most executives and managers state that they are actively changing their IT systems to become more competitive, while only 7% state that they are making only minimal use of IT.

This is a change in the attitude of many managers. During the 1980s, a debate was carried on as to whether IT contributed to productivity. Figure 11.4 shows that not only do executives believe that IT systems contribute to productivity but they have understood the underlying construct: that IT can be used to change business processes. Thus, executives are willing to invest in IT to achieve customer satisfaction, improve productivity and profitability and reduce expenses.

Note the differences among the triad regions. North American executives are concerned primarily with customer satisfaction, productivity and profitability, while Asian executives are concerned with productivity and improving the use of information on an infrastructure basis within the firm. European executives are concerned with customer satisfaction and profitability. Time will tell which information strategies generate the most success.

An understandable dichotomy exists in the ways managers describe their organization's set of objectives and investment policies. As Figure 11.5 indicates, the same executives who stated that proactive strategies towards investment in IT are important, have stated that within their own firms they perceive IT as reactive to business strategy. Nearly 30% think that IT is perceived as a driver of business strategy. This represents a lag between the way executives value IT objectives and the way the organization as a whole practises IT investments. Many executives still feel that budget constraints drive IT investment decisions rather than the possibility of increasing business capabilities with IT.

Actively changing IT systems to gain competiveness	53%
Enhancing current IT systems	42%
Changing part of IT systems	30%
Working on main institutional systems	20%
Making only minimal use of IT	7%

Figure 11.3 How companies are adjusting IT systems. (*Source:* The Economist Intelligence Unit.)

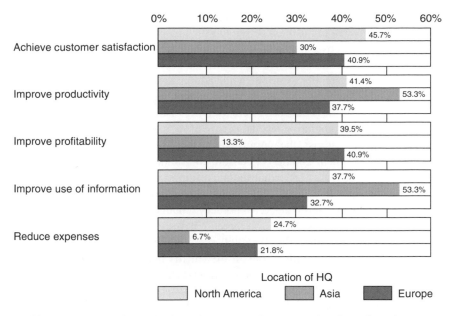

Figure 11.4 Top five objectives that are most important when investing. (*Source*: Economist Intelligence Unit.)

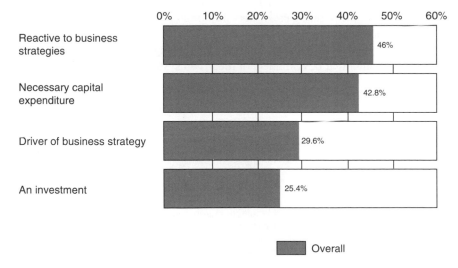

Figure 11.5 How is IT perceived at your firm? (*Source:* Economist Intelligence Unit.)

Still, in Figure 11.6, we can see that by comparing executives responses of growth in business activity to the growth of IT within the business activity, that the coverage of IT within each process is increasing. In other words, for each business activity, more will be accomplished with IT than is currently being done. For example, while administration activities will grow at 17%, the growth in the amount of the task that will be covered by IT will be 20%. Perhaps these executives are thinking of the automation of more clerical functions for tabulating results, the use of scenario modelling for strategic decision-making across the company, or the use of cooperative databases across management functions to ensure coordination.

Managers state that the most important applications for companies over the next five years will be decision support, portfolio management, order matching and routing, cross border exchange of information and on-line tracking.

Managers also see an increase in the amount of on-line, real-time transaction information that they will need. Nearly 80% of managers state that they have critical applications in their firms that require full-time availability of information access. The same amount state that their firm could only carry out activities effectively for less than 24 hours without their critical on-line systems. Nearly all (94%) state that live data is very important to the running of their businesses. In short, business dependence on real-time IT is being recognized by business and IT executives and managers.

Real-time transaction access flow is also aided by the ability to move an application from system to system and to have systems work together. Whereas there has been some decentralization of IT capabilities within companies, the importance of having common management systems and networks on a company-wide basis is important to managers.

Managers think that the time period to see financial benefits from applications should be less than a year. This is in sharp contrast to systems development methodologies of the past that called for multi-year planning and implementation schemes. With the increasing use of fourth generation languages and microcomputers by managers, managers will undoubtedly expand their development of their own systems.

IT growth		Activity growth
20%	Administration	17%
26%	Business communications	24%
26%	Customer services	24%
22%	Distribution/warehousing	21%
20%	Finance	19%
25%	Manufacturing/production	21%
24%	Research and development	20%
20%	Retailing	21%
24%	Sales/marketing	23%

Figure 11.6   Need for IT to grow during the next two years.

Finally, when asked how their IT systems currently fulfilled their expectations, only a small percentage said that they were satisfied (4%). Most answered that their IT systems were average and a fifth considered there was a significant gap between their desire for information systems and the state of the systems they had.

Expected benefits from IT systems are improved customer service, reduced lead time for new products and services, improved overall performance, improved ability to coordinate activities from remote locations, and the improved performance of both operational and managerial tasks.

The changing organization

The single most important condition for success in implementing IT is the commitment from the top of the organization. Executives and managers state over and over again that the leadership, support, commitment and involvement of top executives in IT is fundamental to the continuity of any IT initiative. Clear understanding of IT, enthusiasm of employees, and good functional alignment are the requirements of an organization that is growing and changing.

The responsibility for the IT strategy is changing. More executives mention that a cross-functional team (30%) should contribute to the IT plan, although a full 42% state that the IT department still leads the overall process. Only 15% stated that a central planning department was responsible for the creation of the IT and business strategies.

Decentralization of IT within companies is continuing, with over 40% of companies stating that IT will be decentralized to the user areas by the year 2000 (29% are now), with an increasing amount of the IT expenditure being charged back to business areas as opposed to being supported by corporate overheads. This represents the shift from responsibility of the chief financial officer, who now holds IT responsibility for about 30% of companies, as contrasted with the prediction of 19% by the year 2000. A third stated that IT responsibility will remain, ultimately, with the CEO.

The top five areas in the organization for growth in IT applications are customer service, sales order processing, purchasing, manufacturing and accounting.

Putting it all together

The IT products and services industry is changing as companies' needs for information change. The emphasis is changing from hardware to software and services. New standards for communication are emerging across industries that allow further interorganizational integration. New technologies and ways to manage them will occur. Managers can choose either to work to pull the seemingly chaotic powers of technology together with human skills or to ignore the potentials this wonderful science has to offer.

As we travel to the future, we shall be more involved with managing information and knowledge. Successful future managers and executives will have a significant advantage by taking up the management challenge of information technology.

Action checklist

(1)   Does your company currently have a restructuring project?

(2)   Is your company attempting to become global? What information strategies are supporting this initiative?

(3)   Does your company have access to up-to-the-minute market information on a first hand basis: that is, generated by the company itself?

(4)   How is the organization changing to take up the challenge of information technology?

(5)   In three to five years time, will your company be different because of information technology strategies? Will your career have changed?

References

* The content for this chapter has been derived from two studies conducted for the Economist Intelligence Unit: (1) *Business Strategy 2000: Corporate Strategies, Systems and Service Needs.* The Economist Intelligence Unit, 215 Park Avenue South, New York, New York 10003; and (2) *On-Line Transaction Processing: Enhancing Your Business Strategy*, The Economist Intelligence Unit, 40 Duke Street, London W1A. Combined, these worldwide studies surveyed over 3500 companies and interviewed over 100 business and information executives. For more details, contact the Economist Intelligence Unit.

Daniels, J. L. and Daniels, N. C. (1993). *Global Vision: Building New Models for the Corporation of the Future.* New York: McGraw-Hill

Appendix A
IT services

Appendix A offers a description of the IT services available on the market. There are several reasons why business managers should spend time comparing service providers and product vendors. First, one purchase tends to lead into another. Products bought today should be compatible with products bought tomorrow. Second, there is a great deal of change occurring in the market. What managers buy today will certainly be obsolete tomorrow. Third, there are people with varying degrees of expertise trying to sell products regardless of whether they are appropriate or not. To make the best of these market conditions, managers should know what they have in-house already, and be fully informed about what is available on the market.

Figure A is a diagram of the products and services available. On the left are the more tangible product offerings, and on the right the more intangible, service offerings. Each company will have to buy a mix of these products and services for the IT portfolio.

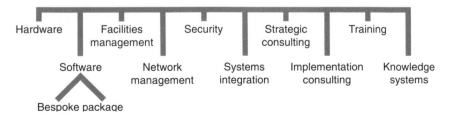

Figure A   IT services.

ware

Hardware vendors provide the processors, memories, drives, controllers, printers and terminals for all sorts of applications. IBM, ICL, DEC, Fujitsu, Apple, NEC, Compaq and Amdahl are but a few. Speciality vendors like Sun Microsystems provide niche hardware, such as workstations, for particular markets. All hardware vendors have very highly trained sales staff. It is important to build a relationship with the vendor to obtain a good discount, but it is equally important to buy solutions for the company's problems rather than try to refit the company to the vendor's solutions. In some cases forming a good relationship with a niche vendor for leading-edge devices can mean that the vendor experiments with new hardware products and services at a company's location. The upside of this arrangement is that the company can find out what is coming on to the market sooner than its competitors, obtain a good discount and, in some cases, help design the hardware to meet its needs. The downside is the time spent testing 'near perfect' equipment. Hardware vendors have one objective: to sell more equipment. One strength to look for in a vendor is the ability to find compatible products and services throughout the range of IT products and services.

Software

Software, the applications that run on the hardware, is available in many shapes, sizes and colours. There are basically two types of software available outside the company: bespoke and package. Bespoke software is written to the company's specifications by the software provider. The company, therefore, gets a system designed to meet its needs.

The problems with bespoke systems are two-fold. First, if the company wants changes made to the system, management must ensure that in-house personnel can handle the changes or that the vendor will be available to provide fast, reliable service at a reasonable price. Second, the company may form a dependency on the software provider in that the more unique the solution, the more time-consuming it will be for the software vendor to maintain the system. Of course, if the software company runs into difficulty, the customer shares that.

If, however, the software vendor is a strong partner, there are several advantages to out-sourcing (developing outside the company). First, the company can get software companies to bid competitively. Second, the workload of the in-house IT department does not interfere with the speed with which the project is carried out. There are a number of vendors who have spent time studying applications with the resources that few companies, on their own, could develop. They may, therefore, have a deeper knowledge of the application issues. Finally, if the company wants to change the software it is not left holding resources that are obsolete.

Package software also has positive and negative aspects. On the positive side, implementing software with packages can be accomplished quickly. The onus is on the user to learn how to apply the software to the company's problem. This can be done by modifying the software with in-house resources, or in partnership with the vendor. The company has the advantage of being able to shop around among different solutions. The negative risk is that the package may not fully meet the company's IT needs and thereby prevent further development of business activities.

Through discussions with vendors on support, maintenance and future upgrade issues, companies can develop valuable relationships with software providers.

Facilities management

This is the area of IT product and services to which the term 'out-sourcing' first applied. With facilities managers, companies can out-source any part of the IT operation that they would prefer another company to deal with. The range is limitless: from the payroll function, to receivables, to the whole computer resource. This was a booming business in the 1980s and is bound to continue well into the 1990s as the price of managing in-house IT resources continues to increase and become more complex. Specialists in data management, hardware, software and integration will manage the operation for companies at a price.

The advantage is that, once again, the customer can shop around for services. The disadvantage may be in the area of security, although in many instances the facilities managers can provide better security than companies can on their own.

Network management

Network management is, in fact, an area of facilities management. However, by virtue of its size of market and its rate of growth, it merits independent attention. As the electronic highways of the future are in the process of being built, there is still a need for private network providers. Networks are expensive. By spreading the costs of the network over many companies, network managers provide fast, reliable service for networks. In future, as more governments become involved, the business will probably look very much like a utility does today, leaving the niche markets, such as high security, for the private providers.

Security

Security is growing almost as fast as the awareness of fraud and disaster. Only 'almost as fast' because companies still have a tendency to leave security issues to the infrastructure projects that somehow never get addressed. Methods of encryption, identification, structuring and back-up are developing more quickly as global networks become more integrated. Estimates are that in future security could take up as much as five per cent of any IT budget.

Systems integration

Systems integrators have stepped in to solve the problem of: 'What happens if all the pieces managers buy do not fit together?' They have appeared from every direction. Hardware and software vendors, facilities managers, and even companies which have developed unique ways of connecting systems offer ways to help companies achieve their dream of 'seamless' computing.

The plethora of operating systems and products continues to grow. Until standardization is demanded by a core group of users the need for systems integration will also grow. Experience in this field used to be limited to those few individuals who had the opportunity to work in several different environments, piecing together many types of technologies. Now, since the need is much more prevalent, companies sensing a market for integrating solutions have focused knowledge resources to solve many of these issues.

Strategic consulting

There is a wide range of quality available in strategic consulting. There are business management consulting firms that have learned a bit about IT, and there are IT strategic consulting firms (not many) that have jumped in and worked out the business strategy issues.

In fairness to the consultants, they are often brought into companies to solve the impossible problems: 'Take two years out of our three-year design cycle', 'Develop a way for us to find out what our customers are thinking', 'How do we grow ten-fold in the next ten years while doubling our profit margin and with the same number of employees we have now?' These are typical assignments for strategic consultants, and it takes a rare breed of problem-solvers to enter this field.

The company's ability to accommodate and manage the consultant's work is vital. It will depend on the strengths and weaknesses of both firms and the seriousness of the problem.

These consultants are undoubtedly the heart and brain surgeons of IT. They are expensive and one slip of the knife can have far-reaching consequences, but they are also capable of saving a company's life or accomplishing all the tasks mentioned above.

Using strategic consultants is not for the faint-hearted. A good way to start is to ask the firm to come in and assess the issues and put together a proposal for carrying out the full solution. Then take a section of the project that both firms agree is an initial module that will benefit even if it is the only leg of the project completed. Spell out the deliverables, the costs and the resources required, then try out the service.

Implementation consulting

Implementation consulting is easier to buy than strategic consulting. The same principle applies in trying out the service: get the picture of the big project and try an initial piece. In implementation consulting, firms will have varying experience in industries and types of issues. Buying experience is worthwhile, buying a solution in search of a problem is not.

Nearly all the major accounting firms now have implementation consulting departments. Ask for a list of projects and specialities and spend time talking to the senior members of the teams. Get as much advice about the company's issues as possible. Be explicit about benefits, costs and timeliness.

Training

Training is becoming an issue for every member of the firm as IT becomes integrated into business processes, as business managers take on more important roles in IT projects, and as new methods and technologies are introduced faster than ever. Although in-house training areas can address much of the ongoing regular training the organization requires, using outside resources to provide new methods and training in new areas is vital to keep the training programmes fresh.

Interactive media and other image-, text- and voice-based systems will become increasingly available from vendors. Some have a vision of each person having a communications platform that can help them determine the amount and areas of training required to face present and future business problems.

The number of firms in this area has risen sharply. Most of the best have links with organizational design and media techniques. Sourcing from many training vendors in the future will no doubt be the norm. Getting to know who's who in the marketplace or going to a training broker will become more common as more business skills rely on continuous learning.

Knowledge-based systems

As jobs require higher skills, some of the knowledge required can be offered to employees via database systems that hold such information as products and services the company offers; ways to handle customer situations; customer histories; who in the company can solve a problem; and how quickly a service can be supplied. Knowledge-based systems (systems that hold data in readily retrievable ways) make it possible for employees to refer to knowledge throughout the organization to help them carry out their activities.

Knowledge-base developers specialize in capturing some of the data that can be shared through databases around the organization. They also develop the systems that will offer the data to employees. Knowledge bases do not replace the need for human knowledge. They provide a way to capture the repetitive information that can be shared throughout the company so that more of the employees' time can be spent on unique problems and issues.

Employees can use knowledge bases to capture information about their own activities to improve the way they work. Interactive training sessions integrated with the person's job will enable him or her to increase skills at individual learning rates in available time.

Knowledge-based systems are designed as tools to help managers capture and manipulate valuable information for their own needs.

Appendix B
The Business
Executive's IT
Bookshelf

Appendix B offers a selection of business management resources that will help managers to understand IT. Rather than being extensive, the list is meant to offer essential sources.

Newspapers and periodicals

Byte

This magazine can get a bit tetchy, but it lists a number of sources for IT products and services and has thought-provoking articles about the industry and business problems. Published in the USA.

CIO

This is a relatively new magazine, but the articles are informative and interesting. Articles are often written from the perspective of the chief information officer (CIO), and describe in detailed anecdotal ways the issues and problems faced by many different types of organization, and how they resolved some of them. It is very readable. Published in Framingham, Massachusetts, USA.

Computerworld

This publication keeps track of all of the major developments in the IT industry. It is published in a newspaper format in Framingham, Massachusetts, USA.

The Economist

Peter Haynes, the current IT editor, combines a number of interesting and innovative themes that always render an insightful look at business information technology.

Financial Times

The coverage Dr Alan Cane and business technology regulars such as Della Bradshaw, Simon Holberton, Christopher Lorenz and Louise Kehoe give both the industry and the business issues is quite superb. Published in London.

Harvard Business Review

If managers read this they will stay up-to-date on all of the latest developments in business IT. *HBR* regularly has leading academic and business leaders who contribute to the leading edge of thought and practice. Published in Boston, Massachusetts, USA.

Sloan Management Review

The magazine covers leading-edge issues in IT in depth. Leading practitioners offer solutions to prevalent IT problems. Published at Massachusetts Institute of Technology in Cambridge, Massachusetts, USA.

Stage by Stage

'Leading edge' practices developed at Nolan, Norton & Co. The articles feature CEOs, CIOs and leading thinkers on global issues of business information management. A surprising number of the methodologies reproduced in consultancies all over the world stem from this publication. Published by Nolan, Norton & Co., One Cranberry Hill, Lexington, Massachusetts, USA.

Executive Bookshelf

Bradley, S. P., Hausman, J. A. and Nolan, R. L. (1993). *Globalization Technology and Competition: The Fusion of Computers and Telecommunications in the 1990s*. Boston, MA: Harvard Business School Press

Bradley, Hausman, and Nolan look to the future and the influence the information highways will have on our businesses and lives.

Cash, J. I., Jr, McFarlan, F. W., McKenney, J. L., Vitale, M. R. (1988). *Corporate Information Systems Management: The Issues Facing Senior Executives*, 2nd edn. Illinois: Irwin, Homewood

If you are going to have one book on your shelf, this should probably be it. This is the Harvard Business School faculty's exploration of IT and business issues. The edition with the case studies is most useful, yet a lot more expensive, because it brings the issues to life.

Davis, S. M. (1987). *Future Perfect* (entitled *2001* in some countries). Reading, MA: Addison-Wesley

This book is primarily about the shift in principles underlying our business assumptions. It is a little difficult to read, but the ideas are well worth it and link threads of thought that have been in the back of most leading practitioners' minds but needed articulation. A thoughtful book.

Earl, M. (1989). *Management Strategies for Information Technology*. New York and London: Prentice-Hall

Professor Earl of the London Business School has compiled the leading issues and paradigms in IT and crafted his own messages throughout this very informative book. A read through this will bring the manager up-to-date with most of the major issues.

Keen, P. G. W. (1991). *Shaping the Future: Business Design Through Information Technology*. Boston, MA: Harvard Business School Press

The telecommunications wizard points to key pivot points in strategic information technology.

Keen, P. G. W., Scott Morton, M. S. (1978). *Decision Support Systems*. Reading, MA: Addison-Wesley series in decision support

For those who want a book that explores the way computer systems can support decisions for managers, this is a fascinating study of the fundamentals. Keen and Scott Morton manage to put their finger on the Gordian knot so, at the least, managers can see the problem.

Rockart, J. F. and DeLong, D. W. (1988). *Executive Support Systems: The Emergence of Top Management Computer Use*. Homewood, Ill: Business One Irwin

This book focuses on the executive use of systems: value, action, reward.

Schein, E. H. (1992). *Organization Culture and Leadership*, 2nd edition. San Francisco, CA: Jossey-Bass Publishers

This is the definitive work on organizational change and how information plays a part in the life of organizations.

Schwartz, P. (1991). *The Art of the Long View*. New York: Doubleday, a division of Bantam, Doubleday, Dell

The Global Business Network leader looks at the value of long-term visioning for executives and managers.

Senge, P. M. (1990). *The Fifth Discipline: The Art and Practice of the Learning Organization*. New York: Doubleday, a division of Bantam, Doubleday, Dell

Senge looks at organizational change for managers and how learning changes with information management.

Stoll, C. (1989). *The Cuckoo's Egg*. London: Pan Books

For every system manager or system manager to be, this book is an account of how one hacker caused havoc on the worldwide network of computers. The book clearly illustrates the need for all of us to take security and intellectual property law seriously.

Toffler, A. (1990). *Power Shift*. New York: Bantam Books

Heidi and Alvin Toffler have put together a series of wonderful books that describe the changes taking place in the world as it moves from the industrial era to the information age. The books *Future Shock*, *The Third Wave* and now *Power Shift* place the changes in business information technology into a daily context that shows the major influences in our lives. An interesting read.

Zuboff, S. (1988). *In the Age of the Smart Machine*. New York: Basic Books

This book attempts to explain what the move to the information age means for managers. Shoshana Zuboff, a professor at the Harvard Business School, explores how the nature of managerial work will change. All students of management information or management science should read this book.

Glossary

Bandwidth   Information can be carried via media within a range of acceptable frequencies. the term refers literally to electronic frequencies capable of
carrying messages for different media. Colloquially it has come to describe
any media that will accept different ways of sending a message. A narrow
bandwidth in this sense means that the media for carrying the message is
restricted in the amount and quality of the information it can convey.

CAD   Computer-aided design (CAD) in its widest sense includes any part of
the design activity that is assisted by computers. Designers use CAD
because of its ability to show designs in three dimensions, to simulate
environments that can test out designs and to change the parameters of the
design quickly. An added advantage is gained when designers from many
countries share an image-based CAD system, yet speak many different
languages. Via the network, the designers can alter designs to 'show' the
other designers on global teams what they mean by the changes they suggest. Seeing the image increases the understanding between multigeo-
graphic teams working together, and helps overcome language barriers.

CASE   Computer-assisted software engineering (CASE) enables software
designers to produce programs very quickly to fill a variety of needs. It is
based on the concept that computer programs that run all the applications
that managers use in business activities are made up of a number of repeatable modules. The CASE method has created a number of these modules
that perform standard functions and a language that helps to manipulate
the modules, so a program comprised of a set of modules to carry out a
function can be put together more readily than by a programmer writing
entire programs from scratch.

EDI Electronic Data Interchange (EDI) refers to systems that exchange data at high speeds via communication lines. Interorganizational systems, such as those shared between customer and supplier, rely on EDI links. The first widespread applications of EDI in business were the shared geological systems associated with tracking seismic activity. These were closely followed by links between banks for electronic funds transfer among financial institutions. EDI now provides links among a wide spectrum of communication applications. Standards for EDI include those established to facilitate high speed integrated data transfer, such as the standardization of bar-coding techniques between retailers and wholesalers to facilitate exchange of commercial data.

Entropy The rule of nature that states that as soon as something reaches a desired state, it begins to decay. In information systems, the moment a system is 'finished' it begins to lose some effectiveness. Since in development the system is aimed at future needs, a system reaches its greatest effectiveness when the picture of the future the system is predicated on is closest to reality. This is likely to ebb after the system is in production for a certain amount of time. The system then requires alteration and maintenance to meet the changing business conditions.

Holism A philosophical term describing the theory that the whole is greater than the sum of its parts. By working as an integrated whole as in a living organism, rather than a series of discrete parts as cogs in a wheel, a company can gain synergistic benefits.

There is increasing interest in defining the added benefit of managing the system as a whole rather than managing it as a series of parts. However, one business executive and owner said: 'As soon as the parts of my company are worth more than the whole of it together, I will sell it off, because this will indicate to me that there is no added benefit to keeping the business together.'

Information technology The branch of computer science and practice that attempts to classify, retrieve and disseminate information. The application of systems of information and knowledge particularly as applied to business and learning. The hardware and software apparatus that provides the electronic structure to support information logic. It is important to distinguish information *technology* from information *systems* (see p.32).

Infrastructure The mainstay systems of any company are commonly referred to as the infrastructure. These are the systems that must run to support all other systems. They include: networks, standards, processing services, training, storage and security. They may also include some standard applications that are used throughout the company, for example Email (electronic mail), voice and image.

ISDN Integrated service digital network (ISDN) is based on the recent breakthroughs of technology including fibre optics, cellular radio, satellite communications, broadcasting and television, artificial intelligence and speech recognition, digital switching and transmission. The combination is forming the electronic highways of the future that will offer instantaneous communication with high visual and audio resolution.

LAN A LAN (local area network) is a network that serves IT facilities throughout one location. A network linking personal computers in a bank would be referred to as a LAN. If a company has two physical locations joined by a network, this is called a connection of two LANs or a WAN (wide area network). Taken to a further level, a network that links many locations is simply called a network, and must either be carried by a private service network provider or by one of the utility companies offering this service.

Manager job family A job family is a group of jobs related by the level of expertise required to fulfil the responsibilities involved and the similarities of the roles the people in the jobs take on. Thus, managers, florists, coal miners, clerks and journalists are all job families.

Pareto rule The business rule of thumb taken from a nineteenth-century Italian sociologist, that colloquially states that understanding 80% of the problem is enough to solve most of the problem.

Real-time Managers' need for immediate responses from IT systems created the phrase 'real-time' during the days of batch or delayed response systems. As a person interacts with a system, the system responds within seconds, causing no interruption to the flow of process the person is carrying out. Most IT systems are operated on a real-time basis since microtechnology has provided distributed processing power.

Value analysis A way of measuring the benefit of IT in an organization. This evaluation technique demonstrates and evaluates the potential of IT to create a 'value chain' of increased productivity, better utilization of resources or the more effective use of information.

Index